ALL THE YEARS COMBINE: THE GRATEFUL DEAD IN FIFTY SHOWS

RAY ROBERTSON

BIBLIOASIS
Windsor, Ontario

FIRST EDITION
10 9 8 7 6 5 4 3 2 1

Library and Archives Canada Cataloguing in Publication
Title: All the years combine : the Grateful Dead in fifty shows / Ray Robertson.
Names: Robertson, Ray, 1966- author.
Identifiers: Canadiana 20230484123 | ISBN 9781771965705 (softcover)
ISBN 9781771965712 (EPUB)
Subjects: LCSH: Grateful Dead (Musical group) | LCSH: Rock musicians—
United States—Biography.
Classification: LCC ML421.G772 R65 2023 | DDC 782.42166092/2—dc23

Edited by Daniel Wells
Copyedited by Martin Ainsley
Cover designed by Jason Arias
Typeset by Vanessa Stauffer

Canada Council
for the Arts
Conseil des Arts
du Canada

ONTARIO ARTS COUNCIL
CONSEIL DES ARTS DE L'ONTARIO
an Ontario government agency
un organisme du gouvernement de l'Ontario

Canada

ONTARIO CREATES | ONTARIO CRÉATIF

Published with the generous assistance of the Canada Council for the Arts, which last year invested $153 million to bring the arts to Canadians throughout the country, and the financial support of the Government of Canada. Biblioasis also acknowledges the support of the Ontario Arts Council (OAC), an agency of the Government of Ontario, which last year funded 1,709 individual artists and 1,078 organizations in 204 communities across Ontario, for a total of $52.1 million, and the contribution of the Government of Ontario through the Ontario Book Publishing Tax Credit and Ontario Creates.

PRINTED AND BOUND IN CANADA

CONTENTS

BONUS TRACK

HIDDEN TRACK

Praise for LIVES OF THE POETS (WITH GUITARS)

"One part of *Lives of the Poets* is a record guide revealing these undiscovered treasures, the other is Robertson's gift of spewing out stories that simply shame most rock 'n' roll writers into the hacks they really are." —*Beat Route*

"Smart, amusing and compelling ... Robertson's writing style walks the line between the scholarly approach of Robert Christgau of *Village Voice* and *Rolling Stone* fame and that of Lester Bangs (*Rolling Stone, Creem,* etc.) who rivaled Hunter S. Thompson in terms of opinionated and decadent balls-to-the-wall journalism. Robertson likes to drop frequent F-bombs to remind us that this is no ordinary academic subject, but he never seems to lose track of the idea his readers are looking for facts and intelligent arguments. He's a genuine rock 'n' roll enthusiast who knows his stuff." —*Winnipeg Free Press*

"There's much to like ... but its real strength is in Robertson's voice, which bobs and weaves throughout each essay ... [His] irreverent voice, his character-driven storytelling abilities, and his personal indebtedness to the lucky thirteen make the collection work. This isn't a history lesson tethered to research— it's a novelist's exploration of pioneers and the high drama of their lives." —*The Alt*

"[Robertson] brings a good ear and plenty of critical insight to essays aimed at helping readers discover new favorites or hear more familiar music from a fresh perspective." —*Kirkus Reviews*

"Robertson has a fine way with words, bringing to bear an insightful mind and a wide-ranging set of influences and perspectives ... He brings his subjects alive with all their flaws and human foibles and makes the reader interested in delving deeper into both their stories and music." —*Penguin Eggs: Canada's Folk, Roots, and World Music Magazine*

To Jim, Dolph, and the Kid Myles

and Dave Lemieux
and Sally B.
and the North Maple Mall

All the years combine
They melt into a dream
—"Stella Blue" (Jerry Garcia/Robert Hunter)

INTRODUCTION

I BELIEVE THAT a Grateful Dead concert is life.

Like life, it can be alternately compelling and lacklustre; familiar and foreign; occasionally sublime and sometimes insipid. A Dead concert—the good, the bad, the so-so—is real because the Dead were real. At least until the late 1970s, the end of their creative peak and the beginning of their gradual transformation into a far-less-inspired and -inspiring arena-rock (and, later, stadium-rock) band, the Grateful Dead were a lot of things, but entertainers wasn't one of them. As rhythm guitarist Bob Weir quipped at the outset of their justly legendary February 13, 1970, show at the Fillmore East, *This ain't a show, it's a party.* What you heard, in other words, is what you got: the Grateful Dead, in all of their maddening, if endearing, mercurialness, intermingled with their astonishing ability to acquaint the listener with the miraculous. They wore to their gigs what they wore to the grocery store. They eschewed show-business babble onstage (and weren't averse to spending a stupefying amount of time tuning up between tunes). They were accustomed to introducing and developing new songs in concert, in front of paying audiences, the process of playing

13

them live aiding, they claimed, in their discovery of what they should ultimately sound like. Consider this: Weir essentially learned how to play slide guitar *on stage*. What other band—or its fans—would allow, let alone encourage, such a thing? The relationship between the Grateful Dead and Dead Heads was profoundly symbiotic. Sure, there wouldn't be Dead Heads without the Grateful Dead, but there also wouldn't have been the Grateful Dead—not as we came to know it—without Dead Heads.

As with any group of musicians who collects fans and followers, the Dead has its share of fanatics, those whose number-one commandment is *Don't be a hater*, and whose determining critical compass is that *It's all good*. Which, of course, it's not—it's *not* all good. Nothing, anywhere, ever is. And how fortunate for us. Without the dark, it's impossible to see the light, and without acknowledging the shrunken musical stature of the Dead in its creatively declining years (which were, by far—and certainly not coincidentally—its most commercially and financially successful era) is to necessarily diminish the astounding and always-evolving artistic expansiveness of the band at its peak.

It's doubtful whether Thomas Carlyle would have dug the Dead—most cranky nineteenth-century Scottish moral reformers didn't—but he knew the importance of critically separating the rock-and-roll wheat from the blah-blah-blah chaff, of judiciously differentiating between what's just okay and what's absolutely necessary. From *On Heroes, Hero-Worship, and the Heroic in History*: "All deep things are Song. It seems somehow the very central essence of us, Song; as if all the rest were but wrappages and hulls! The primal element of us; of us, and of all things." But—and it's an essential *but*, the *but* that brings the necessary light—just "as we love the true song, and are charmed by it as by something divine, so shall we hate the false song, and account it a mere wooden noise, a thing hollow, superfluous, altogether an insincere and offensive thing." Well, maybe not offensive, but certainly subpar and, worst of all creative crimes, sort of boring sometimes. Who has time for what's dull? Not the astutely living, and certainly not the insensible dead.

Although well-meaning and entertaining tribute bands continue to proliferate (one of which included three of the surviving members of the group), the Grateful Dead stopped the day Jerry Garcia's heart did, August 9, 1995. What remains, however, is the next best thing to being there in the third row, courtesy of the group's uncommon decision near the outset of their existence to record their concerts. And, in some ways, it's actually preferable. An ill-timed concert bathroom break can result in a missed musical moment, but if you're listening at home, all you need to do is press the pause button. Additionally, if it's a special moment, you can listen to it again and again and, along the way, perhaps even discover subtleties and associations not picked up on the first time around. Keeping the focus on the music also serves to help keep the focus on what matters most: the music. Now that the Grateful Dead have become subsumed by mainstream culture (file under: Hippie Nostalgia), there's no lack of Grateful Dead–themed nights at hockey games or cute Jerry Garcia bobbleheads or commemorative drinking glasses and key chains, but at the expense of obscuring the main reason to still pay attention to them nearly thirty years after their final performance: the music. Sociology is okay; art is better.

Bear—Owsley Stanley, the Dead's original soundman and early financial benefactor—claimed that the idea to tape the band's gigs had been his, to help him with his onstage mixes and to give the neophyte group a chance to hear how they performed. And while not every show is in the band's famous vault—shit happens, even when you're documenting the divine—the vast majority of the group's 2,350 concerts are. It's possible, then, for someone to follow the band's evolution (and devolution) primarily through their live shows, from the R&B-based garage band at the beginning to the jazz-rock conjurers at their creative peak to the lumbering, MIDI-manacled monolith of their decline.

Which is what this book is about: who the Grateful Dead were, what they became, and what they meant—*musically*. And continue to mean. I also believe that listening to the Grateful Dead will make you a better person. Not just a more knowledgeable listener, but a happier, more enlightened human being. "Look lovingly on some object," the Zen student is advised. "Do not go on to another object. Here, in the middle of this object—*the blessing*." If you hang around the numinous long enough, don't be surprised to find magic in your muesli. Be grateful. That's what art does.

This ain't a show, it's a party.
—Bob Weir, 2/13/70

7/29/66 – PNE *Garden Auditorium, Vancouver,* BC

Standing on the Corner; I Know You Rider; Next Time
You See Me; Sittin' on Top of the World; You Don't Have
to Ask; Big Boss Man; Stealin'; Cardboard Cowboy; It's
All Over Now, Baby Blue; Cream Puff War; Viola Lee
Blues; Beat It On Down the Line; Good Mornin' Little
School Girl

BEFORE THEY WERE a band, the Grateful Dead were friends,
San Francisco Bay Area friends. Jerry Garcia was a banjo-
picking bluegrass obsessive; Bob Weir was a teenage folkie;
Bill Kreutzmann, a jazz-loving rock-and-roll drummer; Phil
Lesh, another jazz fan, who wanted to compose contemporary
classical music; and Ron "Pigpen" McKernan liked to sing the
blues. Before they were the Grateful Dead, though, they were
the Warlocks. And before that, they were Mother McCree's
Uptown Jug Champions.

Jug music is sort of the genial idiot offspring of old-timey
music and bluegrass, music not nearly as technically demand-
ing as the latter (one of the key instruments, after all, is a jug),
but with a foot-tapping exuberance to it that's sometimes absent from the former. Plus, unlike bluegrass, which, live, tends
to attract mainly other fanatical pickers, and folk, which by
the mid-'60s was slowly losing its cultural cachet, there was
at least a chance you could attract enough of an audience to
occasionally get paid to perform. People giving you money to
have fun is a powerful incentive to keep doing it.

Then the Beatles saved rock and roll and made it okay for
young people to like it again. Garcia had listened to R&B radio
and early rock-and-roll records as a teenager and grown up

worshipping the dominant six-string slingers of the day (Chuck Berry, Bo Diddley, James Burton), and it didn't take long for Mother McCree's Uptown Jug Champions to morph into the Warlocks (and, not long after, the Grateful Dead, because it turned out there was already a band called the Warlocks), a rock-and-roll group with bluesy overtones (think early Rolling Stones—basically, a cool cover band).

Eight months before the release of their self-titled debut album—by 1966, everybody in San Francisco with long hair and an electric guitar was getting a record contract, because none of the record companies wanted to miss out on signing the Next Big Thing—the recently christened Grateful Dead (Garcia had discovered their new name while flipping through a dictionary) performed their inaugural international gig at the rather lamely dubbed "Vancouver Trips Festival." It wasn't only the name that was feeble. After the band is announced to a few claps and a long belch of silence, bassist Lesh can be heard to quip, "Our fame has preceded us." Fuck it. Let's go. Hit it.

Opener "Standing on the Corner" is an illuminating distillation of the group's musical makeup at this embryonic stage of its development. A group-penned composition, the lyrics are anti-establishment, sub-Dylan pedestrian; the music, Stones-inspired, garage band–basic (Pigpen handling the de rigueur Vox Continental organ), Garcia's lead vocal unconvincingly strident and sneery. Weir, who would eventually metamorphose into an exceptionally unique rhythm guitarist, is virtually absent in all the clamour (perhaps for the best), and Lesh is still busy learning the basics of the instrument he'd taken up only twelve months earlier. (Garcia, who'd asked Lesh to join the band, didn't let the fact that Lesh had never played the bass before get in the way of good vibes and shared musical sensibilities.)

Even Garcia's guitar playing, while competent, of course, and the primary point of instrumental interest, is more a collection of influences than the inimitable, endlessly inventive, crystalline wonder it would become. (He'd exchanged his banjo and acoustic guitar for an electric guitar only a little over a year before.) What they sound like is what they are: a bunch of guys learning how to play their instruments and how to use their voices and how to write songs. All four group originals performed on this night—energetic, rudimentary, endearingly dated—would fit right in on any *Nuggets* compilation. (Tellingly—and commendably—none of them made it to vinyl and all of them were soon dropped from their live shows.)

It's the covers, which make up the majority of the set, that are the most satisfactory. Garcia is at his best as a vocalist singing electrified old folk songs like "I Know You Rider" or Dylan's "It's All Over Now, Baby Blue," songs that are as enduringly effectual lyrically as they are attractive melodically. (It's a testament to his taste that, although he was no writer of words himself—as evidenced by his few, self-confessedly amateurish attempts—he instinctively knew what worked and what didn't.) Pigpen, on the other hand, sounds pretty much exactly as he would for the entirety of his tenure with the band, his confident takes on blues tunes like "Big Boss Man" and "Good Mornin' Little School Girl" revealing him to be the group's most accomplished performer (and recipient of the most applause, if still conspicuously sparse). This cuts two ways: Pigpen arrived fully formed—a show-stealing, rabble-rousing blues belter—but he never aspired to be much more and was still singing, and still singing well, most of his earliest efforts until he was permanently forced from the band in the summer of 1972 due to alcohol-abetted health reasons. ("Next Time

You See Me" and "Big Boss Man," both included here, were also performed on the Europe '72 tour, his last). In retrospect, it's as if he was keeping the customers happy until the rest of the band could catch up.

The festival's organizers and some of the hipper attendees were undoubtedly aware of the Dead's extensive Acid Test history. Because let there be no misunderstanding: no drugs, no Grateful Dead. Most of the band members had been smoking marijuana for a while, and LSD, which was legal in California until 1966, was simply the next logical step in experimenting with inspired illogicality. Lesh claimed in his memoir, *Searching for the Sound: My Life with the Grateful Dead*, that everybody in the band except Pigpen took acid once a week or more during the three months or so that the Acid Tests were going on. It's helpful to remember that the band didn't get paid to play at Ken Kesey's legendary LSD-laden happenings—each of the Warlocks handed over their own dollar to get in, just like everybody else who attended—and the traditional performer/audience dichotomy was rendered almost nil. Sometimes the Warlocks would play. Sometimes—too high to concentrate (excepting Pigpen, who stuck to booze— unless he got dosed)—they'd set down their instruments after a few minutes and simply watch whatever other craziness was going on around them. And sometimes, emboldened by acid's delightful dismantling of time and prescribed structure, they'd flirt with that most challenging, yet most rewarding, of group musical activities: jamming.

The borderline cacophonous "Cream Puff War" (with lyrics almost as embarrassing as its title) isn't exactly jamming, but it edges toward the real thing. At times, "Cream Puff War" sounds like the Seeds backing up a guest guitarist intent upon replicating Mike Bloomfield's part on "East-West," Lesh, for the first time all night, stepping away from his timekeeping duties and giving us a tasty taste of the signature assertive bass playing to come. "Viola Lee Blues," a jug band tune from the 1920s (another old-timey chestnut resurrected by the Dead, courtesy of Garcia's encyclopedic knowledge of folk and bluegrass) rides ascending notes to another "East-West"–like tension/release clamorous climax, a long (ten-minute), minor-league, modal romp.

After more muted applause, it's back to the band's strong suit, another Pigpen-sung blues, Sonny Boy Williamson's "Good Mornin' Little School Girl." Pigpen nails it, naturally, but pay attention to the group between numbers, listen carefully to who calls out most of the tunes and who keeps things moving along. Pig might be the featured attraction, but this is clearly Garcia's show, even if it's more than a couple of years away from becoming the band it could and would be. At one point, tired and hot and thirsty, Garcia says that if somebody out there isn't too busy, maybe they could bring some Cokes up to the stage. It's nice to think they got them.

10/22/67 – *Winterland Arena, San Francisco,* CA

Morning Dew; New Potato Caboose; It Hurts Me Too;
Cold Rain and Snow; Turn On Your Lovelight; Beat
It On Down the Line; That's It for the Other One (i.
Cryptical Envelopment; ii. The Other One; iii. Cryptical
Envelopment) (set list incomplete)

ANOTHER DRUMMER, ANOTHER gig, another step closer
to who they were supposed to be. The audio evidence is incomplete, but everything you need to know about the state
of the Grateful Dead's collective musical consciousness in the
late fall of 1967 is right here, a benefit concert for themselves.
(Why not? They played enough fundraisers for other people.)
The band and a bunch of their friends may have been busted for
marijuana possession a few weeks previous (even poor Pigpen,
who never touched the stuff), but this didn't slow them down
musically. At this point, *nothing* slowed them down musically.
And not just because the group's idea of goofing off was practising eight hours a day or gathering in somebody's hotel room
after the gig to critique that night's recorded performance.
Hippies worked for a better world; beatniks wished the world
would just go away. Don't be fooled by the long hair or the
occasional tie-dye couture: the Grateful Dead were beatniks.

It wasn't only that the group had added another set of limbs
in second percussionist Mickey Hart, whose first show with
the group had been three and a half weeks before (Hart had
fallen in with Kreutzmann, the band's other drummer, who in-
vited him along to jam with the group, and in typical Grateful
Dead fashion, he simply stuck around). Initially, Hart com-
plemented the band's new exploratory direction, adding inter-

esting percussion touches and aiding Kreutzmann in keeping things moving when the music got especially spacey. Because of Lesh's non-rock background and disinclination to merely keep the beat—at his peak as a player, he would become the Thelonious Monk of the bass guitar—he didn't cover the bottom of the band's sound like most bass players are expected to, so Hart helped anchor the Dead's music at its cosmically flightiest. The band was also in the process of both shedding its R&B-based cover-band skin (the songs were getting longer, louder, and stranger) and preparing to record its second album, *Anthem of the Sun*, which it determined was going to reflect its exciting new sound. Exciting, but often—*often*—ungainly.

First-set opener "Morning Dew," which would later become one of the group's most affecting numbers, hasn't yet found its properly funereal pace—is almost folk-rock chipper—and Garcia sings the words like he's trying hard to convince the listener how very angry he is that human beings now possess the capacity to blow up the planet. Most "protest" music fails because it's of the self-righteous, fingerpointing variety (*we're right, they're wrong; we're good, they're bad*), and art is never one-dimensional. Not real art.

Almost as distracting is the drumming. Especially on the more rhythmically knotty numbers (like "That's It for the Other One," making its debut here), eights limbs are better than four for delivering the unusual time signatures and overall percussive bedlam. But because Kreutzmann tends to play slightly behind the beat, while Hart is apt to rush it (or annoyingly revert to marching band–style *rat-a-tat-tat* tedium), plain old tidy time-keeping can sometimes be an issue, as it is on "Morning Dew." The problem wasn't nearly as pronounced when it was only Kreutzmann behind the kit, and on the slipperier

stuff he could always swing with an Elvin Jones–inspired proficiency (although still capable of occasionally turning the
beat around just fine, all by himself). Combined with Lesh's
aversion to hanging around the pocket for too long, however,
whether featuring one drummer or two, the Dead were much
more adept at rolling than rocking.

"New Potato Caboose," a Lesh composition with lyrics by his
poet friend Bobby Petersen, is what it is: unattractive musically
and self-consciously "poetic" lyrically, really just another opportunity to chordally jump around and jam, and not in any particularly interesting fashion. (Later, once Garcia found his voice as
a guitarist, at least there would be his scintillating solos to keep
one interested during even the most *ho-hum* composition.)
Although "Caboose" would make it onto *Anthem of the Sun*, it
isn't any more appealing in its studio form, and was dropped
from the band's live shows after a dozen or so performances. Its
most notable feature is what it reveals about the group's desire
for more interesting and "open" ways to play, and the need for
someone (*please*) to compose some non-cringeworthy lyrics.

Pig reliably delivers "It Hurts Me Too" (electric-guitar neophyte Garcia sounding like a very talented beginner figuring
out the blues); "Cold Rain and Snow" is too fast, and Garcia is
still acting the part vocally; "Turn On Your Lovelight" builds
up some steam but has yet to open up (although Garcia does
get a little spacey during the "Let it shine" refrain); and "Beat
It On Down the Line" (a remnant of the band's pre-Warlocks,
Mother McCree's Uptown Jug Champions jug-band days) is
frantic fun and pretty much the way it would sound for the rest
of the band's career.

"That's It for the Other One" is where we first glimpse the
glory of what the Grateful Dead would become. Garcia's book-

ending "Cryptical Envelopment" is intriguing melodically but a write-off, words-wise (he wouldn't put pen to paper again), and would eventually be severed from the body of the song. The other part, though, "The Other One" (a collaboration between Weir and Kreutzmann), even in its infancy is a raging beast, a relentlessly pulsing foundation upon which Garcia and Lesh flirt and fight and follow each other up and down the necks of their instruments. Even here (before Weir has figured out all the lyrics and added his own uniquely slashing rhythm-guitar contribution), the sheer power of the thing and the musical tension throughout are sizzlingly palpable. They weren't quite cruising the cosmos yet—at its best, "The Other One" is right there with "Dark Star" and "Playing in the Band" as an extraterrestrial jamming vehicle—but their eyes were on the stars, and they were speeding in the right direction.

2/14/68 – *Carousel Ballroom, San Francisco,* CA

1: Morning Dew; Good Mornin' Little School Girl; Dark
Star>China Cat Sunflower>The Eleven>Turn On Your
Lovelight

2: That's It for the Other One (i. Cryptical Envelopment;
ii. The Other One; iii. Cryptical Envelopment)>New
Potato Caboose>Born Cross-Eyed>Spanish Jam;
Alligator>Caution (Do Not Stop on Tracks)>Feedback;
In the Midnight Hour

WELL, SOMEONE'S BEEN busy. Very, very busy. A bunch of
new songs, some fresh new ways of performing a few old ones,
and a full-time lyricist, Robert Hunter, an old bluegrass buddy
of Garcia's (among the bands they shared membership in was
the Hart Valley Drifters). Hunter was not only an improvement on what the band had previously been capable of, word-
wise, but he'd improve over time as well, his lyrics becoming
as emblematic of the band's music as Garcia's guitar or Lesh's
bass. Since his friend's forming of the Warlocks, Hunter had
dropped out of the folk scene; acquired and conquered a speed
habit; joined and quit the Church of Scientology; like Garcia,
experimented with psychedelics; and by the time he ran into
Garcia again in San Francisco, was devoting most of his time
to scribbling rock lyrics, something that the literate Hunter
(unlike most people in the Dead's universe, he preferred Joyce
to Tolkien) would never have thought worthy of his effort, if
not for what Bob Dylan had recently done to help legitimize
the place of words in contemporary music.

Hunter mailed Garcia the lyrics to something he called "Alli-

gator" and not long afterward received a letter in return saying that the band had set the words to music, and that Hunter
should join them in San Francisco and bring along some more
lyrics and start working with the group directly. "Alligator" was
the only Hunter co-written song on 1968's *Anthem of the Sun*,
but it wouldn't be long (by the time of their third long-player,
the following year's *Aoxomoxoa*) before the songwriting credit
"Garcia/Hunter" was as ubiquitous in the land of the Dead as
the skull-and-roses logo. (The Dead were unusual in that, with
few exceptions, neither Garcia nor Weir wrote the words to
their own songs, the former working with Hunter, the latter
mostly with John Barlow, a childhood friend.)

The group also now had its very own performing venue,
the Carousel Ballroom (co-leased and co-managed with the
Jefferson Airplane, the Quicksilver Messenger Service, and
Big Brother and the Holding Company). So what if—because
beatniks tend not to make good business decisions—the club
would be a bust and shut down within six months? Two of the
new tunes they played tonight would become Grateful Dead
perennials, the band was evolving musically, and the new lyricist was just as committed to his craft as the musicians were to
theirs. Well, most of the musicians... In any case, the official
opening of the Carousel Ballroom was Valentine's Day, 1968,
and the Dead played a sweetheart of a gig.

"Morning Dew" is better for being less. It's still wonderfully, brutally energetic—as is the entire gig, a hallmark of most
shows at this time—but it's more intense for holding something back. (When a keyboardist in his band told Miles Davis
that sometimes he didn't know what to play, Davis told him not
to play anything, then. In time, Garcia would come to recognize the value of playing fewer notes and toning down the vocal

emoting—and start singing more like he was speaking, rather than declaiming, the result being that his voice would grow to be as powerful and effective an instrument as his guitar.) "Good Mornin' Little School Girl" might be just Pig doing his best Sonny Boy Williamson, but the harmonica breathes fire and the drums are everywhere and the clanking guitars are a jerky joy, the kind of instant ecstasy that only comes from long hours of practice, practice, and more practice.

"Dark Star" makes only its fourth appearance, and it's tempting to call it "Dark Star Jr": it's already melodically beguiling, but also startlingly speedy, a mere six minutes long and not yet a jamming vehicle (and Pigpen's predictable little organ chirps and percussive stabs are as good an indication as any that the band needed a keyboardist who played less monochromatically and who liked to wander up and down the keys). It even lacks the defining opening four-note twin tingle of Lesh's bass and Garcia's guitar. What it does have is Hunter's lyrics.

Which aren't poetry, of course (lyrics need music to swing; poetry doesn't, the music comes included), but are a wonderful complement to an already-mesmerizing musical husk, rarely diverting the listener's attention as had been so cringingly often the case in the past. For Garcia, more important than anything else, words had to fit the music. Hunter's words *fit*. "Dark Star" still had some musical growing to do before becoming the mighty interstellar oak it one day would be, but this is the otherworldly acorn where it all began.

But wait: "Dark Star" segues into the second-ever "China Cat Sunflower," another new Hunter-penned lyric (nascent stutter-step rhythm and wavering phrasing and uncertain key included, Garcia attempting to sound "poetic" much like he's trying to sound "outraged" during "Morning Dew").

But wait: "China Cat Sunflower" segues into "The Eleven" (the crisp and clean but slightly miraculous transition soon to become a Grateful Dead hallmark), also only its second appearance, the goofy words and slightly embarrassing Elizabethan vocal stylings forgivable for the relentless, surging rhythm and Garcia and Lesh's joyful jamming (even if still a little mid-range mushy due to Weir's and Pigpen's comparatively bland contributions).

But wait: "The Eleven" segues into "Turn On Your Lovelight," what a rapturous set-ending way to remind everyone that all spaceships eventually return to Earth.

The Dead had played a bunch of shows with the Charles Lloyd Quartet back in the spring of '67, and the saxophonist and his boffo band of musicians (Keith Jarrett on piano, Cecil McBee on bass, Jack DeJohnette on drums) opened up the band's ears to the notion of linking tunes together, particularly longer, more-improvisational songs. This wasn't anything new to jazz musicians, but rock bands playing non-stop for an hour was; the Dead were ripe for the hint. At their peak a few years later, the Dead would take jamming farther than it had ever gone in the popular music field before or since, genuine rock-and-roll gestalt. It's interesting here to recall Garcia's long apprenticeship in bluegrass, which is an intensely collaborative art form, where, if the musicians aren't actively listening to what each other is playing, the music tends to become static and formulaic. Which is precisely what happened to the Dead a few decades later, when age, addiction, and simple apathy eroded the band's probing, pioneering spirit. (The Grateful Dead rarely even had a set list when playing live; the group would know the evening's opening tune, and that would be about it, as the evening progressed Garcia or Weir or Pig just

feeling the need to play this or that song and the band dutifully striking it up. They also never indulged in any showbiz
smarminess—never introduced themselves from the stage, for
example, or addressed the crowd en masse, unless it was to
"Take a Step Back," when the audience at the front of the stage
was being squished.)

How hot was 2/14/68's second set of segued songs? Most
of the remainder of the show—all but "Spanish Jam" and "In
the Midnight Hour"—was utilized by the band for their next
album, the maverick concert/studio mash-up *Anthem of the
Sun* (and in the same order they were played here).

That's *still* not how hot it got, though—as good as all this was
(including an absolutely unhinged "Alligator"), a very spacey
"Spanish Jam" might be the evening's highlight. Still not con-
vinced? "That's It for the Other One" includes a newly written
second verse, the one about Cowboy Neal at the wheel. Appropriately, just before the start of the second set, Garcia dedicates
the rest of the show (which was being broadcast locally) to the
line's namesake, Neal Cassady, Kesey associate and Kerouac's
model for *On the Road*'s anti-hero Dean Moriarty, who had
died six days before. In the succeeding onstage chatter, someone (it sounds like Pigpen) says, "Neal ain't dead, what are you
talking about?" Listen to this show and you'll agree.

2/11/69 – *Fillmore East, New York,* NY

1: Good Mornin' Little School Girl; That's It for the Other One (i. Cryptical Envelopment; ii. The Other One; iii. Cryptical Envelopment); Doin' That Rag; I'm a King Bee; Turn On Your Lovelight; Hey Jude

2: Dupree's Diamond Blues; Mountains of the Moon; Dark Star > St Stephen > The Eleven > Drums > Caution (Do Not Stop on Tracks) > Feedback > We Bid You Goodnight

E: Cosmic Charlie

AN OPENING ACT they were *not*—whoever the headliner was, the Dead demanded their due and were never anybody's idea of a nicely innocuous warm-up band—but on this night they were. And what do you know? The Grateful Dead could almost be professional if they had to be. Almost. Being grownups wasn't one of the band's many collective strengths.

Back in the fall of '68, for instance, the biggest musical problem the group faced was Weir's and Pigpen's lack of musical chops, the latter's especially. As Garcia's and Lesh's own instrumental abilities were increasing, so did their musical ambitions. Why root around in the blues with Pig when they could soar through the stratosphere as psychedelic aviators? (That Pig didn't do drugs wasn't the problem; Weir, whom the band also deemed technically deficient, had taken his fair share of LSD trips.) So Garcia called a meeting and attempted to ease the two stragglers out of the band. Sort of. Weir's inability to play a consistent rhythm part, which Garcia needed to continue to progress as a lead guitarist, was discussed. The topics of Pigpen's indifference to the newer, extended, improvisatory material and his unwillingness to practice his instrument were broached. And here's what's so Grateful Dead about the entire thing: the meeting ended, and no one knew for sure if they were still in the band, not only Weir and Pigpen, but anyone else in the group. What happened was the two musical delinquents slunk off and took some music lessons (Weir eventually developing into an unorthodox but highly original and effective rhythm-guitar player); the other members formed a live side group, Mickey and the Hartbeats, that played only the more complex music they'd become so smitten with (with only so-so results); and a month or so later the entire band was back together on stage. That's the Grateful Dead as applied to the body politic: nobody gets kicked to the curb—c'mon, it's Weir, it's Pig—but everybody pulls their weight, each according to his or her own abilities.

It may not have been an ideal solution—according to tour manager Sam Cutler's memoir, *You Can't Always Get What You Want: My Life with the Rolling Stones, the Grateful Dead and Other Wonderful Reprobates*, Pig remained bitter about the attempted coup for the rest of his short life (he *was* the group's original front man, after all)—but it is quintessential Dead: ignore the problem, in the hope that it will either go away or resolve itself. The plus side of this is that the Dead didn't worry about following organizational policy (they didn't have any) or being consistently professional (they prided themselves on embodying the opposite) or keeping their eyes on the prize (psychedelics had taught them that worldly success was mostly a distracting illusion). On the debit side, the Grateful Dead might have been real-deal ambassadors of such '60s ideals as free love, cheap drugs, and free-form rock and roll, but they could also be downright juvenile when it came to managing everyday human relationships. It's not surprising to learn, for example, that although the entire band was at the meeting in question, Garcia had asked manager Rock Scully to do the actual sacking of Weir and Pig. If you're intent upon firing your friends, at least have the decency to do it yourself.

On 2/11/69, the Grateful Dead's friend Janis Joplin was making her highly anticipated post–Big Brother and the Holding Company solo debut, and who better to give the national media and curious New Yorkers a taste of that vaunted San Francisco Sound (whatever that was) than her scruffy old pals, the Grateful Dead. According to most fans, the press, and Joplin herself (who said afterward that she should have opened for the Dead), her featured act's horn-driven, soul-revue-style show was a little underwhelming. But the Grateful Dead were dependably the Dead, and they delivered, albeit in bite-sized dimensions.

Joplin played an early and a late show, and the Dead did the same, each opening slot scheduled to last no longer than one hour—quite a change of pace when one of their customary second sets could last twice that long. But they managed, emphasizing their blues-and-R&B side, Pigpen (Joplin's old beau and boozing buddy) dominating an opening set heavy on grease and lust and guts, long, gritty versions of "Good Mornin' Little School Girl" and "Turn on Your Lovelight" supplying the bulk of the early show. They also found time to play a tight "That's It for the Other One" as well as debut "Doin' That Rag," a new tune from their album-in-progress, *Aoxomoxoa*. It's different from the sort of thing they'd previously cooked up in the studio—it's an actual song, you can actually hum it—but it was weird enough to still be the Dead. It sounds like nothing so much as a seriously dosed barbershop quartet, and must have been remarkably difficult to perform (it starts, it stops, it charmingly *la de dahs* for a while, it starts and it stops again), which was probably one of the reasons it didn't survive the year as a concert number.

Maybe the most uber-Dead moment of the entire evening is the early show–closing "Hey Jude." After an interminable delay (while Garcia replaces a busted guitar string, the entire band decides it's a perfect time, just before the break, to tune up), Garcia eventually announces that they're going to try something they'd been fooling around with and see what happens (to which Lesh ominously adds, "It might work."). It doesn't— they're using Wilson Pickett's vocally combustible rendering as a template, and Pig simply doesn't have the pipes to pull it off—but considering that Joplin and her management were shooting for major mainstream success by this point in her career (reporters from such middlebrow mainstays as *Time*, *Newsweek*, and *Life* were there to cover her new band's performance), for the Dead—*the opening act*—to haul out a tune they hadn't quite figured out how to play yet, just because it might be fun to give it a shot, is a decidedly uncommercial move. And very, very cool.

The Dead's portion of the late show comprises mostly truncated versions of their increasingly standard second-set fare of interconnected, jam-friendly songs ("Dark Star" > "St Stephen" > "The Eleven" > "Drums" > "Caution (Do Not Stop on Tracks)," but preceding them, and actually opening up the set, are two more songs making their first concert appearance. And goodness Grateful Dead gracious, what's this? Shade and light, yin and yang, thank Christ, thank Buddha, thank Garcia and Hunter, who wrote both of them (and, testimony to their blossoming songwriting partnership, wrote all of the songs on the upcoming album, with only a little help from Lesh on "St Stephen"): acoustic guitars and songs that are actually *about* something and have beginnings and endings and verses and choruses (at least compared to even-less-conventional *Aoxomoxoa* fare like "What's Become of the Baby?" and "Rosemary"). "Dupree's Diamond Blues" is nothing special as a song; based on the old folk song "Frankie Dupree," it could pass for a turn-of-the-twentieth-century jug-band tune, and its most impressive features are Garcia's bemused vocal delivery (he's clearly having a blast recounting doomed Dupree's tale of wedding-blues woe) and recent addition Tom Constanten's calliope-sounding keyboard. (T.C., as he was known, was a university buddy of Lesh's, brought in to cover for Pigpen's lack of keyboard chops as the music became less and less R & B-based and more and more complex). And the sweet strum of the acoustic guitars and the appealing singsongy melody are a refreshing change from the usual amplifiers-on-ten sound. "Mountains of the Moon" suffers from another ostentatious, overripe lyric from Hunter—it's rarely a good sign when you drag kings and queens into your song three-quarters of the way through—but Garcia's arrangement, all rich, billowing acoustic guitars and stately harpsichord-like keyboard, courtesy of T.C., is a mesmerizing, melodious thrill, particularly the chorus, which lacks only the right words to go with it.

After the spaceship lands and the feedback fades and the final notes of "We Bid You Goodnight" have been sung, there's even time left over for an encore of "Cosmic Charlie." You can only hear part of it, though: the tape ran out before it was finished. How Grateful Dead. How perfect.

2/27/69 – *Fillmore West, San Francisco, CA*

1: Good Mornin' Little School Girl; Doin' That Rag;
That's It for the Other One (i. Cryptical Envelopment; ii.
The Other One; iii. Cryptical Envelopment)

2: Dupree's Diamond Blues; Mountains of the
Moon>Dark Star>St Stephen>The Eleven>Turn On
Your Lovelight

E: Cosmic Charlie

ANOTHER WAY OF saying that necessity is the mother of
invention is being in debt to your record label to the tune of
$100,000 (the rough equivalent of three-quarters of a million
dollars today), being contractually obligated to make another
album (and hence incurring even more debt), and eventually realizing that the cheapest and simplest way to make that
happen would be to record a bunch of shows and piece together the new LP from the best-sounding cuts. Which is just
what the Grateful Dead did, the end result being *Live Dead*, a
double-album chronicle of their four-night stand (February
27–March 2, 1969) at the Fillmore West.

Not that failing finances were the sole reason for the album's
genesis. Everyone, not least the band, knew that live was where
they were most Dead, so the idea of capturing the group in
concert on wax had been percolating for awhile. All four nights
were recorded (and recorded beautifully, by Bob Matthews
and Betty Cantor, the always avant-audiophile Grateful Dead
becoming the first rock band to make a sixteen-track recording
of a live performance), and although each night has its high-

lights, the first, 2/27/69, is the one that includes the justly re-nowned version of "Dark Star" that made it onto *Live Dead*, first side, first cut. For many people, it's the definitive Grateful Dead moment from this period. It doesn't occur often, but it does occasionally happen: for a change, many people might be right.

Because the band knew most of the key tracks they want-ed to include on their upcoming LP—the longer, linked pieces they'd been developing for months now, particularly "Dark Star," frequently the centerpiece of their recent shows, which had previously appeared only as a ridiculously pithy 45 (2:44!)—there's an uncharacteristic homogeneity to the set lists across all four nights. (By '73 they could play three shows in three nights with very little set list repetition.) That said, if they did play the big "Dark Star">"St Stephen">"The Eleven" sequence every night, that also meant that they played the big "Dark Star">"St Stephen">"The Eleven" sequence every night. They played Pigpen's showstopper "Turn On Your Lovelight" during all four concerts as well, and on February 27 they closed with it. They also opened the show with another Pig standard, "Good Mornin' Little School Girl," R&B and the blues the nice-and-nasty bun that holds together the psychedelic meat that is the Grateful Dead circa early '69.

Another thing that the Dead were at this time was one with their audience: they looked like each other and lived like each other, and a Grateful Dead show, particularly one taking place in their hometown, was a gathering of the tribes, consecrated by plenty of pot smoke and a healthy suspicion of authority. Listening to the band's shows through the years, it's striking how garrulous Garcia could be amidst like-minded Heads in a reasonably sized venue, particularly since, after the band started playing to larger and larger and less-discriminating audiences in less and less-suitable venues (hockey rinks and, later, football stadiums) he's almost entirely—and very conspicuously—silent. Which makes sense: if you don't know the people you're talking to—if you can't *see* the people you're talking to—why are you talking to them? Showbiz etiquette is not a beatnik virtue.

On this night, after "Doin' That Rag," and nearing the end of yet another instance of the usual tuning tedium that accompanied any Dead show during any period, Garcia (who sounds like he's tripping) feels compelled to let his fellow freaks in on just how different it is to be the one up onstage, as opposed to the one sitting in the audience, just one person trying to convey to a bunch of other people what it would feel like if the roles were reversed: "It's too weird, man, it's really too weird up here, it really is. If you'd like to spend an idle half-hour sometime, you know, just come up here under these similar circumstances and see what it's like. It's truly weird. Beyond the pale." (How anti–rock star is that?) After which, the band blasts off into a set-ending "That's It for the Other One," Lesh's molar-rattling bass more than compensating for the overwrought, over-sung "Cryptical Envelopment" bookends, which would soon be shorn from the body of the indomitable "The Other One." Weir hasn't evolved into the extraordinarily unique rhythm guitarist he eventually would, but Garcia and Lesh (with a little help from T.C.'s organ) ensure that it's a typically enthralling experience.

Second-set openers "Dupree's Diamond Blues" and "Mountains of the Moon" showcase the band's recent, more song-oriented approach, and the brief transition from the latter into "Dark Star," all delicately picked acoustic guitars and a gentle, almost-but-not-quite-recognizable melody, is exquisitely lull-ing—until Garcia takes up his electric guitar and *do do do do, do do do do*, it's ignition time, destination "Dark Star." "Dark Star" changed through the years, as the Dead changed through the years, and this is the age of full-on outer-space explora-tion, the instrumental subtleties all shimmering space-ship silver and black-hole beatitude busyness. This one is a mere twenty-one minutes long, but it packs everything that makes "Dark Star" great during this period into a jamming junkie's dime-bag wet dream.

The "Dark Star" > "St Stephen" from this night were hot enough to be selected for inclusion on *Live Dead*, which ended up doing exactly what they'd hoped it would: publicize their new music and get them out of debt to the record company. And the subsequent raging half-hour of "The Eleven" > "Turn On Your Lovelight" aren't too shabby, either. Let it shine, let it shine, let it shine ...

11/8/69 – *Fillmore Auditorium, San Francisco,* CA

1: Good Mornin' Little School Girl; Casey Jones;
Dire Wolf; Easy Wind; China Cat Sunflower>I Know
You Rider>High Time; Mama Tried; Good Lovin';
Cumberland Blues

2: Dark Star>The Other One>Dark Star>Uncle John's
Band Jam>Dark Star>St Stephen>The Eleven>The Main
Ten>Caution (Do Not Stop on Tracks)>Feedback>We
Bid You Goodnight

IF THEY'D COME to freak out, they'd come to the right place.
What could be freakier in 1969 than the Grateful Dead, the
greatest psychedelic band going (whose lysergic-laced masterpiece, *Live Dead*, would be released two days later), tearing
into "Mama Tried," Merle Haggard's number one country hit of
the year before? How about road-testing five songs in the first
set that they not only hadn't recorded yet, but hadn't even finished writing, songs that sounded even dustier and down-home
than country-and-western kingpin Merle's twangy ode to his
poor old Mama? When they rewarded their ever-patient fans
by playing their standard, jam-filled, spacey second set (and
then some), the otherworldly glow of "Dark Star" must have
seemed like a candle in the window to lead the faithful back
home. When freaky is normal, normal can seem pretty damn
freaky. And in an era when long hair and rock music equals good
people, and short hair and country music equals bad people,
the Grateful Dead performing a Merle Haggard song is freaky.

Since *Aoxomoxoa*, Hunter and Garcia's songwriting hadn't
so much evolved as belatedly begun. "Dupree's Diamond Blues"

and "Mountains of the Moon" were songs, admittedly, but they weren't particularly memorable ones, mainly because, lyrically, they were about as clear as the mud at Woodstock (where, a couple of months before, in a steady rain, the Dead had endured pesky equipment problems and performed so indifferently that they refused to appear in the movie or on the soundtrack). Musically, while undoubtedly intriguing, they tended to go in one ear and float right out the other. There'd been earlier flashes of what was to come—"Doin' That Rag" and "Cosmic Charlie" showed Hunter's nascent witty way of making pleasant nonsense sound perfectly profound when wedded to a couple of Garcia's more memorable early melodies—but the deluge of first-class songs that the pair came up with was certainly unexpected. Unexpected and exhilarating.

So exhilarating, in fact, that after Pigpen gets the evening off to a nice-and-nasty and so-far-normal start with "Good Morning Little School Girl," it's "Casey Jones" then "Dire Wolf" then "Easy Wind," one, two, three, a trio of brand-new neo-bucolic beauties all in a row. As old folkies, both Hunter and Garcia knew Harry Smith's *Anthology of American Folk Music* inside out, front to back, and Garcia, from his bluegrass days, was thoroughly familiar with a whole other tradition of enduring old-timey songs (and as far back as the Warlocks had been keen to include turn-of-the-twentieth-century jug-band tunes in the band's repertoire), but these new songs, while clearly indebted to both men's pasts, were something new. Hunter went on record to say how much Robbie Robertson's work on the Band's first two albums made an impression on him—not to mention the omnipresent influence of Bob Dylan—but the reason why the wry paranoia of "Casey Jones" or the amusing angst of "Dire Wolf" are so clearly superior to what he'd written before is that the psychedelic aspect isn't cartoonish, isn't merely stated anymore, is instead made manifest in characters and stories and setting. "China Cat Sunflower" is deservedly part of the Grateful Dead canon (those familiar opening notes alone are enough to elicit goose bumps), but without the slinky melody and tick-tock tempo cooked up by Garcia, it's mostly just quasi-Joycean gibberish mixed up with some laughably dated hippie conceits. Sung, they're appositely wonderful; read, they're what people who don't know anything about poetry believe poetry is: a bunch of words they don't know saying something that doesn't make much sense.

But they *are* sung (and on *Workingman's Dead*, where they'd all eventually end up, often in sparkling three-part harmony) and were set to music by Garcia to do so, and the country-folk ("Dire Wolf"), bluegrass/Bakersfield ("Cumberland Blues") and straight country ("High Time") influences dominating his songwriting at this time don't feel phony (unlike, say, the Rolling Stones' flirtation with country music around this time, which is near parodic). Garcia not only knew this music, it was his first love, so as a composer, when he turns his hand to it in earnest for the first time, it sounds so authentic it frequently seems like the songs have been around forever. It's almost as if, now that he'd found his voice on the electric guitar, it was okay to go back to the acoustic music that had first inspired him. Several other members of the rock and roll fraternity began to revisit their rootsy roots at the end of the sixties as well (the Byrds, Buffalo Springfield, et cetera), but few had such legitimate credentials.

And just in case anyone thinks that the Dead were once *that* who then became *this*, the second set—the *entire* second set, nearly an hour and forty-five minutes—is one continuous psychedelic squall, a raging electrical storm that includes a taste of a nascent "Playing in the Band" during "The Eleven" and only ends with the a cappella rainbow that is "We Bid You Good-night." Somehow they even find time in the middle of "Dark Star" to dry-run another new tune, "Uncle John's Band," albeit only instrumentally. It sounds pretty great, too.

12/12/69 – *Thelma Theater, Los Angeles,* CA

1: Cold Rain and Snow; Me and My Uncle; Easy Wind;
Cumberland Blues; Black Peter; Next Time You See Me;
China Cat Sunflower > I Know You Rider; Turn On Your
Lovelight

2: Hard to Handle; Casey Jones; Mama
Tried > High Time; Good Lovin'; (I'm a) King
Bee; Uncle John's Band; He Was a Friend of Mine;
Alligator > Drums > Alligator > Caution (Do Not Stop on
Tracks) > Feedback > We Bid You Goodnight

MORE SUCCESS MEANS *more*—more money, more atten-
tion, more opportunities—but it doesn't necessarily mean *better*.
Live Dead, which had been released to exceptional reviews and
brisk sales a month before, did what it was supposed to do—
encapsulate on vinyl the band's growing in-concert powers and
help to pay off a big chunk of the group's ballooning debt to
Warner Brothers—but gigs that had been booked long before
the big breakthrough still had to be honoured, including three
successive nights at a small club on LA's Sunset Strip. A *very*
small club. The kind of club where the people on stage and the
people in the audience are able to kibitz back and forth, and the
musicians can order drinks from the bar between songs, and
after the show is over, if the roadies need a hand, there's always
somebody hanging around who's happy to help out—the kind
of club that the Dead couldn't afford to play anymore. Congratu-
lations, folks, you've finally made it. Welcome to the big leagues.
　　December 12, 1969, was the last of the three dates, and while
there's no "Morning Dew" or "Dark Star" or "St Stephen" or

"That's It for the Other One" (the first of these played on opening night, the latter three the evening before), 12/12/69 is
both special and representative, anyway. "Representative" can
cut both ways. The band was preparing to enter the studio to
record *Workingman's Dead*, and as with any typical gig at this
time, they played a show heavy on newly written numbers,
the band road-testing all but one of the album's eight eventual
tracks. They hadn't left behind their jam-happy past entirely,
however, and treated the assembled to an especially unhinged
"Alligator">"Drums">"Alligator">"Caution (Do Not Stop on
Tracks)">"Feedback" to close out the show. Also typical, unfortunately, are the drums, which are often an undisciplined
mess, the sound of two popcorn machines competing to keep
the beat. Puzzlingly, it's on the much simpler, newer country and folk-based material that the beat tends to get turned
around and the tempos turned inside out. (Although "China
Cat Sunflower">"I Know You Rider" suffers from the same
maddening inability to pick a tempo and stick to it.) The vocals
are rough in places as well, but that's to the group's credit, finding the right phrasing and figuring out what to do with the
background parts a much higher priority than performing
more polished older stuff in place of what needs working on.
Which is precisely the kind of thing you can get away with
when you're playing in front of a couple hundred fellow freaks.
What's a little off-key harmonizing between friends?

It's always instructive to hear how the Dead's songs evolved
in concert, and 12/12/69 provides plenty of opportunities to
do just that, although in some cases "evolved" isn't the right
word. "High Time," for instance, is treated much, much slower here (as are many of the songs; even "Drums" is taken at
an unusually leisurely pace) and is that much better for it, the

awkward, rhythmically-pinched quality of the studio version ironed out live. (Interestingly, another country-rock classic cut in the same unusual 3/4 time signature, Richie Furay's "Kind Woman," which he first recorded with the Buffalo Springfield, was deemed by its author to be rhythmically unsatisfactory and re-recorded at a simplified, slower pace on his next band's—Poco's—*Deliverin'* LP). The swirls of organ supplied by T.C. to the *Workingman's Dead*'s material works surprisingly well, giving the new songs less of a traditional country-and-western feel (as on the album) and more of an old-timey, weird-old-America feel, more akin to something off *The Basement Tapes*. (The calliope-like organ he applies to only the third-ever "Uncle John's Band" and the spooky shades he adds to a decelerated "Dire Wolf" are highlights. As is Garcia's slippery soloing on the former.) Although T.C. would amicably exit the band within six weeks to pursue other musical projects and didn't participate in the *Workingman's Dead* sessions, he was obviously sympathetic to the new neo-country direction, and it's interesting to consider what his decidedly un-country organ sound would have brought to the record if he'd stuck around.

Maybe because they'd shot their longer-song load the previous two evenings, Pigpen picks up the slack and sings a lot tonight, his standout performance not the mammoth (thirty-two minute) "Turn On Your Lovelight" to close out the first set, but a spooky "(I'm a) King Bee" that's dominated by steamy organ and menacing harmonica, Garcia's customary featured guitar uncommonly spare but still stinging.

Pig also handles the vocals on the night's big jamming vehicle, "Alligator" > "Drums" > "Alligator" > "Caution (Do Not Stop on Tracks)" (Garcia chasing down his bliss during his suite-long soloing and conjuring up some astonishingly moody moments), but that's only because the band couldn't figure out what else to play. Literally. After no one onstage is able to come up with a tune to play that everyone can agree on, Weir asks the audience for requests. For real. *Can-you-think-of-something-to-play-because-apparently-we-can't* real. Someone calls out for "Mama Tried," but after what sounds like Lesh not-so-kindly reminding them that they'd already played it ("Yeah," Garcia piles on, "where were you?"), and someone else predictably requests "Dark Star"—and Lesh briefly, jokingly obliges with the famous opening four notes, only to have Garcia *shhh* him with a "No, no, come on"—Pigpen just says, "Alligator," and everyone wordlessly agrees, puts their hands to their instruments and begins to play. It's really that simple. It can be, anyway.

2/13/70 – *Fillmore East, New York,* NY

1: China Cat Sunflower>I Know You Rider; Me and My
Uncle; Dire Wolf; Smokestack Lightning

2: Monkey and the Engineer; Sadie; Wake Up Little
Susie>Black Peter; Uncle John's Band; Katie Mae

3: Dark Star>That's It for the Other One (i. Cryptical
Envelopment; ii. The Other One; iii. Cryptical
Envelopment)>Turn On Your Lovelight

E: We Bid You Goodnight

IT'S HELPFUL SOMETIMES to remember that the health
and happiness of youth have their downside as well. All of
that natural energy and enthusiasm can't compensate for living long enough to understand that, no matter how energetic
and enthusiastic you are, something is going to get in the way
at some point and mess things up, usually something you can't
do a whole heck of a lot about. (See the unfolding career of the
Grateful Dead, for example.) Wisdom is what we get in place
of the joy of making the mistakes that make us wise. That this
might just be sour grapes stomped into elderly-berry whine
is not only possible, but likely. We want what we're not, even
when we get what we wanted. Thankfully, youth knows nothing of this, and would deny it even if it did. Full steam ahead
and damn the torpedoes is what being young is for. Fortunately.
Otherwise, how else could a show like 2/13/70 exist?

This is the Dead the day before Valentine's Day, 1970: savour-
ing the success of *Live Dead* (not only a clear critical triumph, but

their first record to sell in numbers sufficient to satisfy their corporate overlords at Warner Brothers); in the midst of recording *Workingman's Dead*, a collection of country- and folk-influenced, bejewelled beauties that would give the band yet another mode of musical expression (and their first taste of quasi-mainstream success); and booked for two consecutive nights at the Fillmore East, their east-coast home away from home.

Garcia being Garcia, however, this still wasn't enough action—he also had to attempt to learn an entirely new instrument. Garcia being Garcia, he also started playing his newly acquired pedal steel at some informal gigs with an old friend, John Dawson, because music was most fun when performed with like-minded musicians (Garcia was a musical polygamist—he needed different people to play with to keep him stimulated and happy). It wasn't long before he was good enough to guest on other people's albums (that's his distinctive pedal steel guitar on Crosby, Stills, Nash & Young's "Teach Your Children"). Psychedelic space music; twisted Americana; country-and-western songs; naturally, Garcia next had to get involved with organist Howard Wales, every Monday night at San Francisco nightclub The Matrix, to play free-form jazz (where he also met bassist John Kahn, who would become Garcia's chief collaborator outside of the Grateful Dead). Then, after Wales dropped out, Garcia started another band with the former's replacement, Merl Saunders. Saunders was also an organist and, although not averse to jamming, more inclined toward R&B, funk, and any tune with a tasty groove. As long as the music was good—as long as it was fun—Garcia was game.

Speaking of fun, 2/13/70 gets started with a rousing "China Cat Sunflower" > "I Know You Rider," a tune of the band's own, wedded to a song so old no one knows who wrote it, linked together by an instrumental segue that's often the high point of the whole thing. Clearly, this isn't just a quick one to get out of the way to get everybody limbered up. The Dead are *ready* to play. The in-progress appearance of what will become one of the key *Workingman's Dead* cuts, "Dire Wolf," serves notice to those who showed up because of the psychedelic lollipop that is *Live Dead* that this is a group who believes that only if they're engaged and having fun will everybody else have a chance to be as well. And, boy oh boy, is that chorus ever catchy. If you were expecting another short-and-snappy number up next, however, too bad; it's time to unleash the Pig: a nearly twenty-four minute "Smokestack Lightning," a slow burner that, once it's fully lit, gives Pigpen ample opportunity to strut his stuff and belt out a sweaty, swaggering version of the Howlin' Wolf classic (Garcia and the boys, in turn, jamming the hell out of a fairly un-jammable old blues tune in odd, angular ways that the Wolf never would have recognized).

And now, what's this? Where are the drums and the electric guitars and all the rock-and-roll rest of it? Back in the last set, apparently. (When one attendee shouts out a psychedelic request, Weir wryly responds, "Yeah, we're gonna play 'Alligator' *right* now.") Bashed-out acoustic versions of "Monkey and the Engineer," "Sadie," "Wake Up Little Susie"—this is about as loose a busking good time as it gets, a nice reminder that this is why people initially picked up guitars and opened their mouths: to sing songs. Maybe the only thing back-to-basics better than playing and singing songs is playing and singing your own songs, which Garcia and Weir do with two more nascent *Workingman's Dead* numbers, "Black Peter" and "Uncle John's Band." Even Pig gets in on the unplugged act and grabs a guitar and belts out Lightnin' Hopkins' "Katie Mae" all by himself.

After another short break, *now* what? Oh. "Dark Star." A highly melodic, thirty-minute-long, whispering, wandering, tender tour through the cosmos, a soft, shimmering "Dark Star" for warm, country-summer nights in the middle of February in New York City. Into a pummeling "That's It for the Other One," the storm after the calm, another half-hour of going where the music takes them (sometimes somewhere inspired, occasionally somewhere insipid, always somewhere exhilaratingly unknown). Into—I'm not making this up: yes, they really have already been playing full-throttle for an entire hour by this point—"Turn On Your Lovelight," *another* thirty minutes of full-on, if slightly more structured, frothy fun, this time with a beat you can and should dance to, Pigpen the pocket-pool preacher keeping the party going until no one has the energy or even the desire to go any further.

Then "We Bid You Goodnight." Two minutes, entirely a cappella, lay down, dear brothers and sisters, lay down and take your rest. Tomorrow is Valentine's Day. The show starts at eight.

5/2/70 – *Harpur College, Binghamton,* NY

1: Don't Ease Me In; I Know You Rider; Friend of the
Devil; Dire Wolf; Beat It On Down the Line > Black Peter;
Candyman > Cumberland Blues; Deep Elem Blues; Cold
Jordan; Uncle John's Band

2: St Stephen > That's It for the Other One (i. Cryptical
Envelopment; ii. The Other One; iii. Cryptical
Envelopment) > Cosmic Charlie; Casey Jones; Good
Lovin' > Drums > Good Lovin'; Cold Rain and Snow; It's a
Man's World; Dancing in the Street

3: Morning Dew; Viola Lee Blues > Feedback > We Bid You
Goodnight

WHAT IS THIS? Why aren't my ears bleeding? Where are the
electric guitars? Where are the drums? Turn it up, man, turn it
way up. Dark Star! Alligator! St Stephen!

To which Garcia, ever so sagely if just a little annoyed, answers, "Everybody just relax, man—we've got you *all* night."

A month before the release of *Workingman's Dead*, the
Grateful Dead brought who they were this week to the campus
of Harpur College, in Binghamton, New York, confusing some,
alienating others, and turning on a whole bunch of other people courtesy of an opening set that was all about acoustic guitars
and ditties seemingly as ancient as the hills, including several
that the Dead had just written and recorded themselves. To
further mystify matters, the show was opened up by the New
Riders of the Purple Sage, an unsigned, shit-kicking country
band composed of dope-smoking, long-haired friends from

the Bay Area and just happening to feature one Jerry Garcia on pedal steel guitar. (And presumably because they didn't have enough original tunes to fill out a full set, Weir also sat in during their fifty-minute-long opening slot to help out on NRPS versions of a few country-and-western numbers semi-familiar to Dead fans: "The Race Is On," "Mama Tried," and "Me and My Uncle.") Sometimes, to get your mind properly blown, you've got to open it up. Open it *way* up.

To begin with, it's just Garcia and Weir on acoustic guitars and Pig merrily honking away on harmonica, the old jug-band tune "Don't Ease Me In" a fitting roots-music segue to an hour of fresh neo-folk ("Black Peter"), neo-country ("Dire Wolf"), neo-bluegrass ("Cumberland Blues"), trad. ("Deep Elem Blues"), and even plain, old gospel ("Cold Jordan"). The only letdown is that Pig doesn't sing anything. He must have been too busy backstage drinking wine and smoking cigarettes. Or perhaps explaining to a circle of curious Binghamton coeds the subtleties of Lightnin' Hopkins' finger-picking guitar style. When the band finishes up with the instantly memorable if uncategorizable "Uncle John's Band" (catchy as the flu and a lot more fun), it all makes sense. Folk, country, bluegrass, traditional material, gospel, whatever: as long as the Dead are playing it—as long as Garcia's guitar, acoustic or electric, adorns it—it's Grateful Dead music. As Gertrude Stein did not say, "The Dead is the Dead is the Dead."

Which meant they were also the jamming junkies of their recent *Live Dead* renown, as is immediately evidenced by the thunderous "St Stephen" > "That's It for the Other One (i. Cryptical Envelopment; ii. The Other One; iii. Cryptical Envelopment)" > "Cosmic Charlie" sequence that blows open the doors to the second set (or third, if you're Garcia). The transition into "The Other One" is so pile-driving spot-on, so tumbling-down-the-mineshaft-of-your-mind tight, it's actually a little frightening, like a crack of lightning that simultaneously startles and awes. It's an "Other One" that's a rare hybrid of the shorter, pummeling versions of the late '70s combined with the way-out space wanderings of a 1972–74 "Other One." Even the concluding "Cryptical" is burnished by extended exposure to Garcia's searching, snarling guitar. (It's obvious by now how the almost Zen-like concentration and commitment necessary to become proficient on the five-string banjo contributed to Garcia's single-note, crystalline-kissed mastery of the electric guitar.) It's probably the definitive version.

But *everything* here is jammed out in the key of ferocious, even Pig's "Good Lovin'" and a so-so-sung "It's a Man's World" (Pig certainly feeling it, but his vocal cords letting him down), and even an ill-advised "Dancing in the Street." Sometimes I think I just don't care for the Dead's discofied version of "Dancing" from the late '70s, but then I'm reminded that even on a cookin' night like tonight, sugary pop and honeyed harmonies aren't what the Dead do best. But Garcia's guitar... All night—*all* night—he plays like a man possessed, just give him a tempo and a key and he's off for the cosmos. Check out the beautifully beguiling chords he conjures up at around the ten-and-a-half-minute mark of "Dancing." At one point, he's playing so far outside, it sounds as if the band is readying to circle back to "Playing in the Band," a tune that hadn't even been written yet.

Then there's the third set (only four songs long and more of an extended encore, but over half an hour in length), which is the Cherry Garcia on the cake. "Morning Dew" has arrived (although I could do without the gong, as would the band, eventually), has found the right forlorn cadence and been shorn of Garcia's previously affected delivery. (You can hear how he's delighting in his newly found phrasing, luxuriating in hitting all the high notes.) This is the fourth-to-last performance of "Viola Lee Blues" and it's easy to see why—it's a good, goony time, with lots of electrical anarchy, but as the band has become more proficient on their instruments, there's just not enough room inside the song to move around—but by the time they drive into the blizzard of feedback that wraps it up, you're too happily fried to concern yourself with what is or is not the right jamming vehicle. The night is electric.

Until it isn't anymore, is just a bunch of voices at the end of a long evening singing "We Bid You Goodnight." Folk, country, bluegrass, trad., gospel, psychedelia, Motown, R&B, white noise—why not a West Indian funeral hymn? Yeah, why not?

2/18/71 – *Capitol Theater, Port Chester,* NY

1: Bertha; Truckin'; It Hurts Me Too; Loser; Greatest Story Ever Told>Johnny B. Goode; Mama Tried; Hard to Handle; Dark Star>Wharf Rat>Dark Star>Me and My Uncle

2: Casey Jones; Playing in the Band; Me and Bobby McGee; Candyman; Big Boss Man; Sugar Magnolia; St Stephen>Not Fade Away>Going Down the Road Feeling Bad>Not Fade Away>Uncle John's Band

SIX SHOWS OVER seven nights—all of them at the gorgeous Capitol Theater, an eighteen-hundred-seat performance space originally opened in 1926 as an upscale cinema—would have been enough to put any band in a good mood. Factor in the debut of six—yes, *six*—new songs, and you've got a downright giddy bunch of amped-up musicians on your hands. Because it's the Dead, though—and because life is life—there was a bomb threat the very first night, 2/18/71, that necessitated the clearing of the entire building before the shivering concertgoers were allowed back inside, and Mickey Hart played his final show with the band for over three and a half years. (According to Hart because of his crippling guilt after his father, Dead co-manager Lenny Hart, absconded with most of the band's money a little less than a year before; according to Kreutzmann in his memoir, *Deal*, because of his fellow drummer's heroin use and consequently substandard playing.) Did I mention the six new tunes? And because it's a Grateful Dead show, there's also the unplanned, the unexpected, the unfathomable. That's life, too.

Set opener "Bertha" is one of those new songs, and in typical Dead fashion it's an engaging embryonic mess (exploding with energy, but marred by a wobbly rhythm and unsure vocal phrasing plus a fair bit of uncertainty over how to end it). And they *opened* with it. Talk about *pluck*. New tune number two of the night, Garcia's slow, simmering "Loser," is close to what it would eventually become, although he's still figuring out where all the words go and it's played a tad too briskly. It's immediately followed by *another* two new songs, Weir's "Greatest Story Ever Told" (*chunka-chunka* clunky and not sure yet what it wants to be) into Chuck Berry's "Johnny B. Goode" (played with plenty of panache, although to what end is unclear, because a 4/4-on-the-floor rock-and-roll band is one of the few things that the Grateful Dead was definitely not).

Perhaps they simply needed more material to fill out the set, as Pigpen sings a mere three songs all night, a troubling indication of the health problems that would sideline him by the end of the summer for nearly four months of recuperation. The second set's sole debut number, "Playing in the Band," is the least developed of all, played at a lumbering, tediously tentative pace and lacking what would become the best thing about it, the jammed-out middle section. ("Playing" and "Sugar Magnolia" are among the final fruits of Weir's brief composing relationship with Hunter; henceforth, his best material would feature lyrics by childhood pal John Barlow.) There are two ways to listen to these in-progress songs: as merely early, inferior versions, or as an absorbing glimpse into the Grateful Dead's compositional process, which quite often took place right on stage, night after night, the artist-audience interaction a significant part of what got added, cut, or modified. It's almost as if you're right there with the band the entire evolving time, hearing some of your favourite songs grow up to be what made them some of your favorite songs.

Although by early '71 the band was playing bigger and bigger venues, 1,800 is still small enough to feel as if you're performing for actual people with actual faces and not an anonymous blob of human bodies. And the audience felt more comfortable as well, although calls for "Viola Lee Blues" and "The Eleven" early on in the first set fell on deaf ears, both tunes having been dropped from the rotation in favour of newer songs months back. (Neither was to return to the band's repertoire, either.) Artistic "progress" is a myth (how would one ever gauge such a violently subjective notion? Is *Sgt. Pepper*, with its orchestra and sound effects, better than the relatively under-produced *Revolver*, or just different?), but there is *change*, just as there is in life, and the Dead were constantly changing, embracing and experimenting with (and fusing together) one fresh musical genre after another (blues, psychedelia, folk, country, jazz, rock). The Dead believed what every real artist believes: if they aren't having fun, chances are the audience won't be either. Not that they didn't play a few of their older songs this night, although an extremely low-key "St Stephen" was clearly another tune they were running out of enthusiasm for, as evidenced by its being dropped from the rotation after only nine more performances (although it would reappear five years later to a rapturous response).

They also played "Dark Star"—in the first set, no less—which is short (only about fourteen and a half minutes) and spare (it's basically just Garcia and Lesh and Weir and the drummers, plus guest keyboardist and friend of the band Ned Lagin, as Pig is mostly absent from the mix), but extraordinary nonetheless, both for the interposed, chilling debut of "Wharf

Rat" (uncertain in places and lacking its moving "I'll Fly Away" ending, but still smoulderingly soulful) and for the theme that Garcia plays around with for four consecutive minutes, post-"Wharf Rat," as the band edges back into "Dark Star." We first hear it, briefly, at the song's three-minute mark, but Garcia too quickly discards it in order to flirt with the melody and engage in some spacey back-and-forth with Lesh; after "Dark Star"'s lyrics have been sung, though, he revisits it and gets down to business. How beautiful is it? For years, Dead Heads have identified it simply as "Beautiful Jam." It has an unmistakable Spanish flavor to it, but it's angular and edgy rather than rococo relaxed; it probes, it pulses, it preens. And then, crushingly, it's back to "Dark Star" and it's gone again, this time for good. That's okay. There's another gig tomorrow night. And another one the night after that.

10/19/71 – *Cyrus Northrop Memorial Auditorium, University of Minnesota, Minneapolis,* MN

1: Bertha; Me and My Uncle; Sugaree; Beat It On Down the Line; Cumberland Blues; Tennessee Jed; Black Peter; Jack Straw; Big Railroad Blues; Brown-Eyed Women; Mexicali Blues; Truckin'; Comes a Time; Playing in the Band; One More Saturday Night; Casey Jones

2: Truckin'; Ramble On Rose; Me and Bobby McGee; Brokedown Palace; That's It for the Other One (i. Cryptical Envelopment; ii. The Other One; iii. Cryptical Envelopment) > Wharf Rat; Sugar Magnolia; Uncle John's Band > Not Fade Away > Going Down the Road Feeling Bad > Not Fade Away

REALITY IS A nice place to visit, but you wouldn't want to live there. The Dead didn't, anyway, which was how, in the fall of 1971, when Pigpen had become even less of a presence behind the organ than usual, because of his declining health, Garcia discovered the Grateful Dead's new keyboardist, even though he didn't know he was looking for him.

Keith Godchaux wasn't a rock and roller—was a classically trained jazz enthusiast, who made a little pocket money playing piano on the San Francisco cocktail-jazz circuit—but when he and his wife, Donna, decided one day that what he really should be doing was playing with the Grateful Dead, their favourite band, they did the only logical thing: showed up at one of Garcia's local solo gigs, and during the set break Donna informed him that her shy, silent husband, Keith, was their new piano player. (This, even though no one outside of the band knew how sick Pig was; in fact, he'd been hospitalized and was off the road at the time, being treated for the liver disease that would eventually kill him.) To which most people would have sensibly replied either, "Uh, thanks anyway, but the Dead's not really looking to hire a new musician right now," or "Even if we were thinking of adding a piano player, we're not in the habit of hiring fans whose wives come up to us in public and announce that they're joining the band." Except that's not what Garcia said; what he said was that the Grateful Dead were having a rehearsal on Sunday and that Donna and Keith should drop by and see what happens. Unfuckingreal. You probably wouldn't have done it, I certainly wouldn't have done it, but that's what Garcia did. The next week Keith Godchaux was the newest member of the Grateful Dead, an addition that would not only help compensate for Pig's diminishing contribution, but would inaugurate what many people, myself included, consider to be the Grateful Dead's greatest era.

Maybe it was because it was Keith's first show and everyone was extra-energized. Maybe it was because the band hadn't played a gig in seven weeks (an eternity in Grateful Dead time). Maybe it was because, between them, Garcia and Weir were set to introduce another whopping six new tunes (all half dozen of which they'd still be playing nearly a quarter of a century later). Maybe it was because the concert was being broadcast on a local FM radio station. Whatever the *why*, the *what* of it was that the Dead put on a very long, very spirited, very good show. And the rookie did what all good musicians and athletes do: he not only played well, but made the other people around him play better too.

Keith's influence was immediately evidenced in the new songs, particularly Garcia's. "Tennessee Jed," with its loopy, loping rhythm (although played a smidgen fast here, in its inaugural outing), and the engagingly herky-jerky "Ramble On Rose" weren't rock and roll, weren't country rock, weren't psychedelic neo-vaudeville, weren't anything easily classifiable. Just call them a couple more great Grateful Dead songs that are that much more unique because of Keith's piano-playing contribution. Although he'd never sound particularly comfortable as a soloist, Keith could be an assertive player when the song demanded it (witness his pounding presence on upbeat numbers like "Bertha" and "Big Railroad Blues"). It was the clouds of cascading notes he brought to the band's more "open" songs, however, that illustrated his true musical gifts and why he was such an ideal addition to this particular group of gleeful improvisers.

Even if he might have overplayed at times during his initial outing—first-night jitters could also explain why the entire band tends to take things a little fast all evening—he was also a master at knowing when *not* to play, something Garcia was equally expert at. (Miles Davis used to regularly admonish his band members, "You don't have to plug every hole.") Until his always-sympathetic playing began to atrophy in the late '70s, due to drug abuse and depression, Keith rivaled Lesh as Garcia's main musical foil, never flashy but at all times tastefully apposite. I'm a fan of the unadorned "The Other One" that the band had been toying with (and soon after, would all but stick to), but here they include its gentler "Cryptical" bookends, and Keith's left harmony hand is every bit as adept as his improvising right, his delicate touch here—and throughout the night—a harbinger of all of the intuitive tinkling to come.

It's not all about the new guy on the piano bench, though: in addition to Garcia's two already-mentioned new numbers, there's his still-evolving "Comes a Time," with a couple of extra verses, as well as two more Weir–Hunter collaborations, "Jack Straw" and the reliable party anthem "One More Saturday Night." Weir's "Mexicali Blues," co-written with new lyricist John Barlow, is most interesting for what it attempts to be— an *oompahpah* gunfighter saga—than for what it achieves, but what the hell, at least you can polka to it, and every song can't be "Playing in the Band." Even "Playing in the Band" can't always be "Playing in the Band"—this one briefly falls apart when Weir messes up the words about halfway through. But if you're going to make a Grateful Dead omelette, you're going to have to break a few songs. Check out the achingly elegiac "Wharf Rat" that flows out of the concluding "Cryptical Envelopment." Or the jubilant "Uncle John's Band" > "Not Fade Away" > "Going Down the Road Feeling Bad" > "Not Fade Away" medley. The rookie sounds pretty good on these ones, too.

11/14/71 – *Texas Christian University, Fort Worth, TX*

1: Bertha; Beat It On Down the Line; China Cat
Sunflower>I Know You Rider; El Paso; Sugaree; Jack
Straw; Big Railroad Blues; Me and Bobby McGee; Loser;
Playing in the Band; Tennessee Jed; You Win Again;
Mexicali Blues; Casey Jones; One More Saturday Night

2: Truckin'>Drums>The Other One>Me and My
Uncle>The Other One; Wharf Rat; Sugar Magnolia

E: Johnny B. Goode

NEVER HAVING BEEN a full-time touring musician before,
Keith's first time out on the road with the Dead must have
been overwhelming at times. How could it not have been? The
music was great—right from the start, it was obvious that his
piano was a perfect addition to the band's evolving sound—
but two days before arriving in Fort Worth to play tonight's
show at Texas Christian University, they'd played a gig in San
Antonio, and the night before that they'd been in Atlanta, and
tomorrow night it's Austin, and two days after that it'll be Al-
buquerque. The Grateful Dead had reached liftoff, and the sci-
ence of inspiration said it was time to soar, not enough sleep
and too many drugs and too much time spent looking out of a
tour-bus window be damned. Like the song says, pick a place
to go and keep truckin' on.

The first set, among other things, is for messing around, trying stuff out—before the band gets into a groove, before the
big second-set jamming gets underway, before the drugs really
kick in. Not that the Dead, and Garcia in particular (singing

with conviction and churning out tasty fills during even Weir's shorter, more musically prosaic numbers), aren't *on* from the first *slam-bang* notes of lead-off track "Bertha," which the band had frequently been opening with, ever since its debut nine months earlier. The "China–Rider" is tight and cooks (especially the transition), "Playing in the Band" is still embryonic but *yearning* to escape its six-minute skin and become the jamming vehicle it would be by the time the group landed in Europe six months later, and "Casey Jones" snorts and sashays as it should.

But there was still time, during an early, first-set technical timeout ("Grateful Dead Standard Time, folks," Weir assures us), to give everyone a Pigpen update ("sick back home") and attempt a goofily ambitious twenty-five-beat intro count to "Beat It On Down the Line" that not surprisingly falls apart (they stop, regroup, and try it again, this time with a more-manageable three-beat count). "Tennessee Jed" is still finding its wobbly legs, is still performed too briskly and on-the-one straight ahead, and the Dead's debut of Hank Williams' "You Win Again," which the group would wisely drop after twenty-one performances, is limp and lifeless, and Garcia strains to hit the high notes. So what? Better luck next tune. "We're gonna take a short break and we'll be right back with you in a few minutes," Weir announces at the conclusion of "One More Saturday Night," only its eleventh performance. Oh, boy.

"Truckin'" is strong and steady out of the gate, an auspicious way to kick off the second set (Weir even gets all of the words right, something that couldn't always be counted on), which is followed by… "Drums." Nearly four and a half minutes of… "Drums." I don't get it—never have—but someone in the audience tonight sure does, shrieks and screams when

Kreutzmann commences pounding away. On the other hand: "The Other One." Without the seemingly pointless *boom-boom* buildup, we wouldn't have the emerging tribal familiarity of Kreutzmann's always-unhurried, always-exhilarating introduction, the instantly identifiable percussive preamble to Lesh's song-starting bass bomb. (Who knows? If drum solos are part of a bigger plan, maybe we are too.)

"The Other One" snarls along nicely—very nicely (Keith contributing some *Tubular Bells*–like tinkling a year and a half before Mike Oldfield recorded his career-defining album)—Garcia and Lesh and Keith each taking turns darting in and out of the limelight, Weir *chunka-chunking* along in his increasingly inimitable fashion to help keep the song somewhat tethered to Earth. (*Someone* besides the drummer has to—Lesh has lit out for the celestial territories, can't be bothered with anything as humdrum as holding down the bottom.) And just to show that this is the real thing—that the band is searching for something, something they won't recognize until they hear it—Garcia gets lost temporarily in some sub-Clapton blues wankery for thirty seconds or so before diving back into the confusion necessary to create something special. This ain't showbiz, folks.

The transition into "Me and My Uncle" is magnificent. Being tight has very little to do with playing this inspired—is necessary but not sufficient—and the way that the throbbing fury of "The Other One" so nonchalantly becomes the dusty little ditty "Me and My Uncle" is equal parts intended and inspired. Which only serves to make the ferocious re-introduction of "The Other One" a few minutes later even more compelling. Plainly, they're not following a plan here, a script or a strategy. When the first melancholy notes of "Wharf Rat" bubble to the surface over top of "The Other One"'s slow evaporation, it's mind melt time. Check out the jam at around the six-and-a-half-minute mark, led by Garcia. Nights like this, it seems as if they could keep playing forever without ever once repeating themselves. Without stopping, it's time for Weir to bring us back to sunshine daydreams and rolling by the riverside and "Sugar Magnolia." When it's all over, they'd been playing for nearly an hour straight. Tomorrow night, Austin.

11/15/71 – *Austin Municipal Auditorium, Austin, TX*

1: Truckin'; Bertha; Playing in the Band; Deal; Jack
Straw; Loser; Beat It On Down the Line; Dark Star>El
Paso>Dark Star; Casey Jones; One More Saturday Night

2: Me and My Uncle; Ramble On Rose; Mexicali Blues;
Brokedown Palace; Me and Bobby McGee; Cumberland
Blues; Sugar Magnolia; You Win Again; Not Fade
Away>Jam>Going Down the Road Feeling Bad>Not
Fade Away

E: Johnny B. Goode

THE NEXT NIGHT—THE *next* night (the vigour of youth,
the virtue of cocaine)—the weirdness couldn't wait until the
second set. After an energetic romp through a bunch of new,
still-evolving tunes (including the unrecorded "Jack Straw,"
plus "Bertha" and "Playing in the Band" from the just-released,
two-month-old live *Skull and Roses*, and "Deal" and "Loser"
from Garcia's first solo album, which wouldn't hit stores for
another six weeks), the spookily familiar *do dodo doo, do dodo
doo* of "Dark Star."

Horny as they were to perform and polish all of these wonderful new songs—and they *are* songs, compact and catchy
and imbued with some of the fruits of Hunter's first real run as
a mature lyricist—there was still room for a first-set trip to the
cosmos, still time to put on their spacesuits and mess around
awhile in outer-spaciness. It's only the band's third "Dark
Star" with Keith on piano, but that's okay—the playing all-
around tentative in places, perhaps (like new lovers exploring

unfamiliar bodies), but delicately spacey, too, the tender tinkle of Keith's piano a wonderful acoustic complement to all of that raging electricity. Settling in for a nice long cruise through the cosmos, though, after only twelve and a half delicious minutes, what's this? "Dark Star" sputters, disassembles, collapses, only to emerge, phoenix-like, as ... "El Paso." "El Paso"?

The Dead performed "El Paso" a staggering 389 times, approximately 17 percent of their concerts. "*El Paso.*" Marty Robbins' "El Paso." It's unclear whether Weir enjoyed playing it as much as he seemed to simply because he really, really liked this little piece of AM-radio melodrama, or because he knew it pissed off a certain percentage of the audience every time they struck it up. (Both are equally honest and legitimate reasons. Artists entertain themselves first, *then* everyone else.) *Bumpteteebum, Bumpteteebum, Bumpteteebum, Bumpteteebum, Out in the West Texas town of El Paso* ... Either way, for me, anyway, it often means time for a bathroom break or time to hit the fast-forward button. But tonight, after the celestial chill of "Dark Star," the clodhopping rhythm of "El Paso" is a shade-into-light delight, the sight of blue-marble Earth after the cold, white nothing of outer space a refreshing change of vista. The Texas Dead freaks in attendance on this night, whether from El Paso or not, wouldn't have had to ingest the psychedelic sacrament to wonder if they were actually hearing what they thought they were hearing. Then, after our hero has fallen, and his love, Feleena, comforts her dying saviour, it's back to the outer limits, nearly eight minutes more of chiming, churning "Dark Star"—a "Dark Star" that packs more spirited electrifying *élan* in its twenty and a half minutes than many much longer versions. The first set ends—surprise, surprise—with another unreleased song, Weir's "One More Saturday Night."

After the intermission, more as-yet-unrecorded tunes (an impassioned "Ramble On Rose" and "Mexicali Blues"), a handful of recently released songs ("Cumberland Blues" from the previous year's *Workingman's Dead*, featuring Garcia at his Clarence White-ish, string-bending best; a "Brokedown Palace" that includes some inspired Garcia lead; a nice and peppy—until it turns righteously riotous—"Sugar Magnolia" from that same year's *American Beauty*), and a lengthy, lively, jam-filled excursion through "Not Fade Away" > "Going Down the Road Feeling Bad" > "Not Fade Away." The band had been playing the encore, "Johnny B. Goode," for about a year by this point and would continue to play it—usually in the all-too-predictable encore spot, as they had the night before in Fort Worth—for the next twenty-four years. They should have dumped it like they eventually did "You Win Again." Unlike their slowed-down, swaying take on "Around and Around," they add absolutely nothing to the Chuck Berry original. Not that they cared. They liked it. They played it nearly three hundred times. Good for them.

12/1/71 – *Boston Music Hall, Boston,* MA

1: Truckin'; Sugaree; Mr Charlie; Beat It On Down the Line; Comes a Time; Jack Straw; The Rub; Tennessee Jed; El Paso; Big Railroad Blues; Casey Jones; One More Saturday Night

2: Ramble On Rose; Me and Bobby McGee; Big Boss Man; Cryptical Envelopment>Drums>The Other One>Me and My Uncle>The Other One; Not Fade Away>Going Down the Road Feeling Bad>Not Fade Away

PIG'S BACK!

It's a partial Pig—he sings only three short songs, and his Hammond isn't anywhere to be found in the mix—but after several months on the sidelines (including an extended stay in the hospital), that's good enough for now, it's nice to have a little grease and grit back in the Grateful Dead's set list. Getting drunk and getting laid (or trying to) might not be especially profound pursuits, but they are indisputable parts of the human experience, and Pigpen was the sole member of the band capable of conjuring up the good, sweet stink of sex and the wonderful imbecility of getting plastered. (Weir's super sleazy "I Need a Miracle" is a first-rate raver, but his latter-day blues excursions tend to be more workmanlike than convincing.) The cosmic and the corporeal both have their obligatory place in life, so ideally both should be represented when the Dead plug in and count off and get down to business. And tonight, for the first time in a while, they are.

Considering that it's Pigpen's welcome-back party, it's ironic that Keith, his ostensible replacement, is the belle of the ball, less than two months into his tenure with the band and already making his tinkling presence a big part of the group's sound. He's everywhere here—sometimes soothing, occasionally scary, always active and invigorating—and his unending energy clearly fuels his fellow musicians (including Garcia, who always thrived on a stage mate's inspired playing, but also Lesh, who's similarly omnipresent this evening, particularly on the show's highlight, the remarkable "Cryptical Envelopment" > "Drums" > "The Other One" > "Me and My Uncle" > "The Other One" medley). But it's not just during this monster second-set sequence of tunes that Keith shines: check out the rollicking barrelhouse piano on "Ramble On Rose" or his gleeful pounding during the show-ending "Not Fade Away" > "Going Down the Road Feeling Bad" > "Not Fade Away" sequence. There's so much more *colour* to the band's overall sound, now, with Keith in the line-up, a multihued, horizontal presence previously lacking in the group's primarily six- and four-stringed attack. Pig (and T.C.) certainly freshened things up now and then with their stabs of earthy organ, but it was only when Keith's busy fingers were added to the musical mélange that things really began to open up, his widescreen vision a key catalyst in their eventual drift toward a decidedly more jazz-rock sound in '73 and '74 that was as frequently out-there as anything even Miles Davis was doing live at the time.

Even at this early stage (only his nineteenth gig) Keith proved to be up for whatever weirdness was thrown his way, and on this night, there was lots of it. After the cumbersome "Cryptical" (which would only be performed four more times before being dropped for over a decade, briefly taken out of mothballs for a handful of performances in 1985, and permanently shelved), there's a tolerably brief drum solo that sets up a pulverizing, vocal-less "The Other One," Keith a cat on a hot tin keyboard, rarely leading the charge (never his unassuming style), but always quick to join in on the delightful pandemonium. This is followed up by some very agreeable spaciness (Lesh especially frisky tonight, even less interested than usual in worrying about anything as humdrum as keeping the beat), followed by the unmistakable twang and gallop of "Me and My Uncle"; except that, no, Weir decides he doesn't feel like singing about what went down in that Santa Fe barroom when those angry cowboys accused his favourite uncle of cheating at cards; he changes his mind and instead belts out the first verse of "The Other One." Which leads to more "Space" and *then* "Me and My Uncle"—again—this time for real, vocals and all. After Weir has absconded with the gold and left his beloved uncle's dead ass by the side of the road, it's back to "The Other One" and more electric extemporization and more (*more!*) Lesh-dominated "Space," until finally, we reach "The Other One"'s last verse. (And, no, you weren't hearing things during "Space"; those are the same basic chord changes Weir would employ in the "Prelude" to "Weather Report Suite," which wouldn't be debuted until nearly two years later.)

The "Not Fade Away" > "Going Down the Road Feeling Bad" > "Not Fade Away" closer is the ecstatic icing on the cake, the only thing lacking being Weir and Pig's reliably boisterous call-and-response vocals during "Not Fade Away." Weir calls, all right—calls and calls until you're surprised he doesn't burst his voice box—but Pig never answers, is nowhere to be heard. It was probably prudent to keep Pig on the sidelines for most of his first night out of his pen; the band had eight shows booked in the next ten days. Life on the road with the Dead—*life*, period—isn't a sprint, it's a marathon.

On your mark, get set, go...

12/31/71 – *Winterland Arena, San Francisco,* CA

1: Dancing in the Street; Mr Charlie; Brown-Eyed
Women; Beat It On Down the Line; You Win Again; Jack
Straw; Sugaree; El Paso; Chinatown Shuffle; Tennessee
Jed; Mexicali Blues; China Cat Sunflower>I Know You
Rider; Next Time You See Me; Playing in the Band;
Loser; One More Saturday Night

2: Truckin'>Drums>The Other One>Me and My
Uncle>The Other One; Jam>Black Peter; Big River; The
Same Thing; Ramble On Rose; Sugar Magnolia; Not Fade
Away>Going Down the Road Feeling Bad>Not Fade Away

E: Casey Jones

IT'S TIME TO talk about Donna. By this point it was obvious that her husband, Keith, who'd been the band's keyboard
player for a couple of months now, was more than just fitting in.
In a group full of innovators—at the peak of their powers, no
other lead guitarist, rhythm guitarist, or bass player working
in the field of popular music sounded quite like Garcia, Weir,
or Lesh—Keith's strength wasn't in his stylistic originality but,
rather, in his endless adaptability. Whatever the Dead's kalei-
doscopic music demanded—counterpoint chording, straight-
ahead pounding, astral-plane tinkling—Keith came up with
the goods. And although it would be a few more months before the quick-witted fluidity of his playing helped facilitate
the band's move toward a more jazz-inflected sound, when it
did happen (roughly '72 through'75), Keith was not only a
key catalyst but a major contributor. It would take Donna a

little longer to find her place in the band, but once she did, her contribution would be almost as instrumental as her husband's. Not that every Dead Head felt the same way.

Donna had been a Muscle Shoals studio singer (contributing background vocals to Percy Sledge's "When a Man Loves a Woman" and Elvis' "Suspicious Minds," among others) before moving to San Francisco (where she met Keith) and was the missing piece to the most engaging and varied vocal mix the Grateful Dead ever possessed. A significant portion of Dead Heads, however, like to complain about her in-concert off-key singing and how her enthusiastic contribution to signature songs like "Playing in the Band" and "One More Saturday Night" was more akin to over-the-top caterwauling. Given the staggering amount of sound the Dead generated in concert, particularly as time went on, it would be surprising if she wasn't off-key occasionally (just like everyone else in the group). Her occasional miscues were simply more noticeable, I believe, because she had the highest, most conspicuous voice. As for her occasional screams and shrieks and screeches, the Dead, even at their best, were fairly vocally vanilla, Garcia and Weir both possessing pleasing, distinctive lead voices, but as a harmonic whole, not adding up to anything especially compelling. Like Keith, who eventually diversified the group's instrumental mix with an array of different keyboard colours, Donna gave the band a much-needed dose of vocal vim.

And this is where it begins: New Year's Eve, 1971, always a holiday hoot when the Dead help say goodbye to what was and hello to what will be. Maybe because it was a hometown gig, the band open with an old Haight-Ashbury hallmark, "Dancing in the Street," a tune they hadn't played in over a year and wouldn't perform again until 1976. You know it's a special night when the opening number includes lots of juicy jamming. On the whole, though, the Dead are still in thrall to their songwriting muse, and with so many great new ones to share, why wouldn't they be? (In a very generous seventeen-song first set, of the eleven original compositions, a staggering eight of them had yet to appear on record.) Plus, c'mon, it's New Year's Eve, and if ever there was a time to put away the spacesuits and pull on your dancing shoes, tonight would be it.

As an extra treat, the band even manages to debut a couple of tunes, Weir's rip-roaring cover of "Big River" and Pigpen's agreeably cheeky "Chinatown Shuffle." Although nothing special as a song, the latter is particularly welcome, indicative as it is of Pig's post-hospital commitment to music-making (another newly written number, the immensely moving "Two Souls in Communion," would debut a couple of months later). Plus, he breaks out "The Same Thing," which hadn't seen action since '67. And it isn't just his own material that shows where his Deadhead is at. Now that Keith's got the keyboard textures covered, Pig is freed up to augment each song as he sees fit, a little percussion here, a little organ there, some background-vocal help whenever a song can use it. The entire set wraps up with Weir's "One More Saturday Night," a tune he'll soon record for his solo album, *Ace,* and to which Donna will add her trademark background vocals, as she does here, her first time on stage with the band.

The second set still contains its fair share of welcomed weirdness: if a thirty-two-minute "Truckin'" > "Drums" > "The Other One" > "Me and My Uncle" > "The Other One" doesn't do the trick, check out the short-but-sinister jam that precedes a very un-NYE "Black Peter." Then it's back to the shorter, song-oriented stuff until we're treated to a scorching "Not

Fade Away" > "Going Down the Road Feeling Bad" > "Not Fade Away" to wrap things up. (The "Casey Jones" encore cooks, too.) The only thing missing is Donna's vocals.

In time, in time...

4/14/72 – Tivoli Concert Hall, Copenhagen, Denmark

1: Bertha; Me and My Uncle; Mr Charlie; You Win Again;
Black-Throated Wind; Chinatown Shuffle; Loser; Me and
Bobby McGee; Cumberland Blues; Playing in the Band;
Tennessee Jed; El Paso; Big Boss Man; Beat It On Down
the Line; Casey Jones

2: Truckin'; It Hurts Me Too; Brown-Eyed Women;
Looks Like Rain; Dark Star>Sugar Magnolia>Good
Lovin'>Caution (Do Not Stop on Tracks)>Good Lovin';
Ramble On Rose; Not Fade Away>Going Down the
Road Feeling Bad>Not Fade Away; One More Saturday
Night

EVERYONE AND EVERYTHING made the trip: the band,
the crew, the office staff, friends and lovers and family, along
with an arsenal of pot, coke, and LSD and a sixteen-track recording machine meant to capture every note of every show
for possible use on a future live album. The Grateful Dead were
going to Europe. They'd made the trek twice before, but only
for solitary gigs in 1970 and '71; this was twenty-two shows
over seven weeks and five different countries. With a couple
of quasi-hit records to their name now, it was time for not only
a well-earned working vacation, but time to spread the skull-
and-roses brand abroad. And play some of the finest music of
their long career. It's rare, but commerce and art aren't always
enemies.

The only problem with discussing any of the shows collectively known as "Europe '72" is that perfection can be predictable. The first few, in England, might have been a tad tentative

in places (in addition to Weir's voice being affected by a not-unpleasing raspiness—apparently several members of the touring party picked up colds on the way over), but it's churlish to nitpick about ecstasy. Ho-hum, song after song performed passionately and with aplomb, Garcia and Weir and Pigpen piling on the top-shelf, shorter stuff for a generous opening set, crammed full of energetic rockers and beauteous ballads and everything in between. Sure, "You Win Again" had worn out its welcome long before they got to Europe, and "Casey Jones" is performed a tad leisurely for a song about cocaine, but shut up and listen and enjoy. Sometimes, as during the spring of '72, even "El Paso" makes sense.

"Truckin'" *vroom vrooms* the second set, and although Weir dependably gets the words wrong and misses his vocal cue on the penultimate verse, it's a confident corker and a splendid harbinger of what's to come. "Looks Like Rain," with Garcia on pedal steel, is excellent—talk about tautologies—but suffers from the absence of Donna's harmony vocals. Many of my favourite versions of Grateful Dead songs—"Wharf Rat," "Looks Like Rain," "Sugar Magnolia"—were performed after Donna's role in the band expanded to include her voice on the majority of the repertoire (she sang on only a few songs per show during the European tour). Just like Garcia's distinctive pedal steel work (he wouldn't sit down again behind the instrument at a Grateful Dead show for another fifteen years), sometimes it's illuminating just to be reminded of what you're missing.

The focal point of the evening is the "Dark Star" > "Sugar Magnolia" > "Good Lovin'" > "Caution (Do Not Stop on Tracks)" > "Good Lovin'" sequence. Over an hour long, the highlights are many, and Pigpen is integral to two of them. Pig

was advised by his doctors not to make the trip to Europe, and
although the travelling must have been punishing for a person
in his fragile condition, he and the band did a good job of not
overexerting him in-concert (particularly in the second set,
where he was usually limited to a single vocal number). Tonight, though, the Pig has broken down the walls of his pen
and is running wild, strutting and snorting his way through a
long and leering and nicely jammed, downright spacey "Good
Lovin'," his usual long-form, first-set piece, before doing his
nouveau-voodoo thing on "Caution (Do Not Stop on Tracks),"
which the band had broken out six days before, at Wembley
Empire Pool, for the first time in a year and a half. It's brief—
not even seven full minutes—but it is a delightful, demented
surprise, nonetheless, a reminder to the Danish audience—
most of whom had never seen the band perform live—of what
the Dead were up to back in their acid-kissed San Francisco
ballroom days, a psychedelic postcard from the past. (Pig gets
in on the improvisational act himself, spontaneously spitting
out the opening verse of "Who Do You Love?", a jive-talking
homage, perhaps, to its author, Bo Diddley, who sat in with the
Dead for a few songs at one of the Academy of Music shows the
band played in New York just before jetting off for England.)
"Sugar Magnolia," even without the powerful uplift that Donna
would later bring to it, is always welcome after a long space trip,
but it's "Dark Star," not surprisingly, that is the show's standout.

The Dead usually alternated nightly between "Dark Star"
and "The Other One" during their European excursion, and
tonight's "Dark Star," like all of them, has its own personality,
is delicately probing, even electrifyingly placid in places. At
around the nine-minute mark Garcia tries something—who
knows what—that results only in some ugly, unpleasant noise,

but such is the band's jamming fervour, the others eagerly come along for the ride anyway, what the hell, let's see where this thing takes us. After thirteen minutes, Garcia teases the listener with the tingling four-note "Dark Star" theme but appears to hit a bum note, which he then proceeds to make a virtue of, by following its off-key lead for a while, another happy improvisational accident. At the twenty-two-minute mark, Lesh picks up the tempo and takes Garcia along with him, the end result this time being something akin to a "China–Rider" transition at its most feelin'-groovy dynamic.

After half an hour, Garcia is still happily adrift in deep space when Weir abruptly cranks out the opening chords of "Sugar Magnolia." The transition is so seamless, initially it's almost as if Garcia is simultaneously still serenading the stars *and* playing his customary twangy lead on Weir's ode to that special someone who makes everything delightful, who's got everything you need. Sunshine daydream in Denmark, oh, yeah.

5/7/72 – *Bickershaw Festival, Wigan, England*

1: Truckin'; Sugaree; Mr Charlie; Beat It On Down
the Line; He's Gone; Chinatown Shuffle; China Cat
Sunflower>I Know You Rider; Black-Throated Wind;
Next Time You See Me; Playing in the Band; Tennessee
Jed; Good Lovin'; Casey Jones

2: Greatest Story Ever Told; Big Boss Man; Ramble
On Rose; Jack Straw; Dark Star>Drums> The Other
One>Sing Me Back Home; Sugar Magnolia; Turn On
Your Lovelight; Going Down the Road Feeling Bad>Not
Fade Away

E: One More Saturday Night

THERE MIGHT NOT have been any snow, but there was
plenty of cold rain. And mud. And rain. And mud. The Bickershaw Festival was the Dead's sole festival appearance during
their European sojourn—an impressive bill that included
the Kinks, Dr John, Captain Beefheart, and old pals the New
Riders of the Purple Sage—and the rain let up by the time the
Dead hit the stage Sunday evening, the last night of the festival.
As if to reward the soggy concert-goers who'd stuck it out this
long, the Dead played for nearly four hours (not including a
lengthy break). And played well. Extremely well. Of course
they did. It was Europe '72.

Bickershaw is a Pig-lover's delight—by the numbers alone,
it was the busiest Pigpen had been all tour, and included not
only such Pig perennials as "Next Time You See Me," "Chinatown Shuffle," and "Mr Charlie," but both of his big numbers,

"Good Lovin'" and "Turn On Your Lovelight." Because he was ill (photographs, and what contemporary concert footage there is, reveal him to be disturbingly gaunt, with big eyes and sunken cheeks), there's less rapping and more spacey jamming, which isn't a bad thing. Especially when he was laying down a sex sermon in the middle of one of his showstoppers, Pig sometimes suffered from the affliction of so many white blues singers—trying to sound like an elderly, turn-of-the-twentieth-century, southern Black man of rural origin. Pigpen grew up in San Bruno, California, and, like Garcia, adored the Beats, as well as being a dedicated chess player and a big fan of 1950s hipster Lord Buckley. Every neophyte artist initially learns their craft by imitating their heroes, but if they're to grow and cultivate their métier, they must sooner or later develop their own singular interpretations and style (as, say, Van Morrison, Captain Beefheart, and Alan Wilson did with their own early blues fixations). Pigpen did eventually discover his own authentic blues voice—witness the atypically understated but undeniably moving "The Stranger (Two Souls in Communion)"—but, unfortunately, only after becoming mortally ill ("The Stranger" was performed a total of only nine times, six of them during the European tour). Not everyone is fortunate enough to become who they were supposed to be.

A circa-1972 show of such astonishing duration must necessarily contain a sizeable number of outstanding performances—there's little point in enumerating them all; just scan the enormous set list and salivate in auditory anticipation—and the Dead's two major showcases also received rare concurrent performances at Bickershaw ("Dark Star" > "Drums" > "The Other One"), only one of a handful of times in their thirty-year performing history that these two monster jamming/space machines were linked together in a single show. The "Dark Star" is brief by the standards of the era (just under twenty minutes), but what it lacks in length it makes up for in inquisitiveness and energy, nothing that the band picks up on and explores leading to anything particularly special, but providing a suitably spacey appetizer to the generous (thirty-and-a-half-minute) "The Other One" feast to follow. Near its conclusion, just as an otherworldly "The Other One" reassembles and approaches touchdown, when Keith follows Garcia up, up, up the scales—*tinkle twang, tinkle twang, tinkle twang*—you really hear what the former's addition to the group provided: another gifted, adventurous playmate for Captain Garcia, someone else willing to boldly go with him where no rock band had gone before.

Because, harbour no hippie utopianism: the Grateful Dead was a democracy benignly ruled by an amiable autocrat by the name of Garcia. Which is as it should be. Miles Davis was another genius who encouraged—demanded, actually—that his bandmates not only support him, but also inspire, challenge, and sometimes change his musical mindset and sound. But he was the boss. Even when he put down his trumpet and conducted from behind a keyboard he sometimes didn't bother playing, he was still the captain of the ship, it was his call when they sailed off and returned home. If you're listening through a decent set of headphones—as vintage Grateful Dead should be heard—isolate Weir's rhythm guitar and marvel at the inventive counterpoint he comes up with, the scrumptious little twists and turns he supplies throughout even the lengthiest number, like "The Other One" at Bickershaw. But it's Garcia he's usually responding to, it's Garcia that's ordinarily the one who inspires him to eschew the ordinary and produce something musically amazing.

But it's not just a twin-monster-song show. The "Sing Me Back Home" that emerges from "The Other One" (total triptych playing time: 64:33) dependably delivers the listener back to planet Earth, "Playing in the Band" was stretching out every night and bursting to become the preferred jamming vehicle of '73 and '74, "Going Down the Road Feeling Bad" is rollicking robust, "Greatest Story Ever Told" bursts out of the gate and never looks back, the "China–Rider" is…Put down the menu and dig in. You're going to be here for awhile.

5/26/72 – *Lyceum Theatre, London, England*

1: Promised Land; Sugaree; Mr Charlie; Black-Throated Wind; Loser; Next Time You See Me; El Paso; Dire Wolf; The Stranger (Two Souls in Communion); Playing in the Band; He's Gone; Cumberland Blues; Jack Straw; Chinatown Shuffle; China Cat Sunflower>I Know You Rider; Not Fade Away>Going Down the Road Feeling Bad>Not Fade Away

2: Truckin'>The Other One>Drums>The Other One>Morning Dew>The Other One>Sing Me Back Home; Me and My Uncle; Ramble On Rose; Sugar Magnolia; Casey Jones

E: One More Saturday Night

TWENTY-TWO SHOWS LATER, here we are, back in England, where the whole thing began seven weeks before. And in spite of how tired they must have been, physically and otherwise, this was no slow fade, not unless four consecutive nights at the Lyceum Theatre is your idea of R&R. Then again, after the entire trip was over, Garcia's only complaint was that the band didn't do enough gigs while they were over there. You're hitting the finish line hard when, on the last of four shows in four nights, after spending nearly two months living out of a suitcase, you play for three and three-quarters of an hour.

As well as the ailing Pigpen acquitted himself throughout the tour, though—singing a few songs every night, doing a little preaching during "Good Lovin'" and "Turn On Your Lovelight," providing dependable splashes of colour with the Hammond

B-3 to complement Keith's jazzy tinkling, giving the Dead their richest sound ever, even adding extra percussion when the organ wasn't required—by tour's end he was audibly running out of gas. The tank wasn't entirely empty—during the band's European finale he sang four short tunes in the first set and was behind the organ whenever called upon—but between the conspicuous lack of any of his longer, more-involved numbers and the less-than-Pig-like snort and snarl when singing the shorter ones, it's debatable how much longer he could have carried on if the group hadn't already been scheduled to return home. May 26, 1972, would be Pigpen's last show (he attended the band's first gig stateside, but his sole contribution was providing some occasional organ). At least it was a good one.

There were a lot of *lasts* on this night, including the final "The Stranger (Two Souls in Communion)," Pigpen's recently composed—and best—composition. It's impossible to listen to Pig's aching delivery and not ache a little yourself, to hear his yearning words of wasted opportunities and lost direction and not wonder what might have happened if he'd lived a little longer (he died March 8, 1973). The last song he sang with the Dead was the peppy "Chinatown Shuffle," another newly written number. Pig's maturing vision and craft might have been too late, but it wasn't too little: "Chinatown Shuffle" was the second-most-performed song during the band's seven weeks of touring; "Mr Charlie" (another new song) the third. Pig didn't fade away; Pig's body just stopped. (After his death, Garcia told friends it was the end of the Grateful Dead. It wasn't, but it was the end of something.)

In a first set that's two hours (*two hours!*) long, it's impossible to highlight all of the highlights without writing a tome. It's apt that the last version of "Playing in the Band" performed on the tour was the longest and spaciest yet, eight minutes longer than its maiden voyage on 4/7/72. This one may top out at only 18:01, but it's not the size of the PITB jam that matters, it's the quality, and this one is especially enticing because of its newness, the wide-open spaces the group was investigating for the first time, the intergalactic frontiers still left to conquer. The biggest thrill in the first set might be the crowd-instigated concluding sequence. After what seemed to be a fine, set-closing "China–Rider," the audience sponta- neously breaks into a Bo Diddley shave-and-a-haircut-two-bits clap-along, which must have amused the band, because they proceed to ride the clapping syncopation straight into Buddy Holly's "Not Fade Away" and take another eighteen minutes, through "Going Down the Road Feeling Bad" and back again, to close the first set. It's not the most energetic or exciting ver- sion of either song performed on the tour, but it is the only one that the audience was responsible for striking up. Just another evening with the good ol' Grateful Dead.

The band must have had some lemonade or maybe even a bottle or two of Coca-Cola during the break, because the sec- ond set opens with a charging "Truckin'" (the version includ- ed on the triple-disc *Europe '72*) and just keeps on trucking on from there, the jam that evolves from the song's comple- tion at around the eight-minute mark unique simply because "Truckin'" was never an ideal jamming vehicle, is more of a groove pushed along by the Dead's signature shuffle style. This jam transcends its origins, however; it's simply rock-and-roll jazz—scorching, spooky, at times even scary—and, like the best jazz, worthy of endlessly revisiting.

Until, after ten minutes of fervent jamming, Lesh's bass announces "The Other One," which percolates for nine feverish minutes before turning into a couple minutes of "Drums," until...Lesh delivers a bass bomb and introduces "The Other One" *again*, as if the first time hadn't been quite ferocious enough. Another twelve minutes of impassioned jamming ensues (at one point, everyone else drops out, and it's just Garcia and Kreutzmann dueling away) until..."Morning Dew." Instead of straining to come up with more superlatives, cue up an early version, like the one from 10/22/67, and marvel at "Morning Dew"'s transformation from impotent protest posturing to anguished elegy.

Until..."The Other One"—for the *third* time—this time to finish what it started, including the last verse and a properly pounding ending.

Until... "Sing Me Back Home," eleven minutes of soothing country-gospel to remind us that we're still here and human—for now, at least. Maybe it's me, but Pigpen's churchy Hammond B-3 sounds extra mournful tonight.

8/27/72 – *Old Renaissance Faire Grounds, Veneta,* OR

1: Promised Land; Sugaree; Me and My Uncle; Deal;
Black-Throated Wind; China Cat Sunflower>I Know You
Rider; Mexicali Blues; Bertha

2: Playing in the Band; He's Gone; Jack Straw; Bird Song;
Greatest Story Ever Told

3: Dark Star>El Paso; Sing Me Back Home; Sugar
Magnolia

E1: Casey Jones

E2: One More Saturday Night

THE DEAD DON'T vote. Or carry picket signs or wear but-
tons emblazoned with slogans or belong to any political party.
At least they didn't when Garcia was young and strong and
steering the good ship Grateful. Garcia would have agreed
with Emma Goldman, who famously opined, "Voting is the
opium of the masses." Actually, what he did say when asked by
an interviewer about his take on the American political system
was something akin to, "I don't think it's a good idea to encourage these people." Which doesn't mean the Dead didn't help
out their friends and neighbours and fellow freaks whenever
possible. Quite the opposite, actually.

On August 27, 1972, the Grateful Dead played a benefit
concert for Oregon's Springfield Creamery, owned and oper-
ated by Chuck Kesey (brother of long-time Dead accomplice
Ken Kesey) and his wife, Sue. The band not only played more

benefits than just about anybody else, they did them in spite of being busier than just about anybody else (the 8/27/72 creamery benefit was preceded by gigs on the 20th, 21st, 22nd, 24th, and 25th). Thoughts and prayers proffered during the evening news or stepping inside a voting booth and checking a box beside a candidate's name every four years might make you feel like a good person; getting on yet another airplane and flying to Oregon and playing a three-hour show in record-breaking heat, when all you want to do is go home and pull down the shades and rest your bones before beginning an arduous upcoming fall tour (fourteen shows over eight states in September alone), makes the world a better place. Opinions and good intentions don't pay the bills, at the creamery or anywhere else.

So the Dead showed up and unpacked and played in the sunshine before approximately twenty thousand people, on a 103-degree (39°C) day, when water was in short supply and their instruments kept going out of tune because of the heat. What they didn't do was lecture the assembled attendees about the need for more and better-supported creameries and how, when the revolution arrived, no one would ever have to worry about yogurt insecurity again. They just played. And played so well that 8/27/72 has become a part of Grateful Dead concert legend. It's a legend that stands up to scrutiny.

It was the fall of '72 (almost), so of course it was going to be a good show. Post-Europe, everything seemed to work: the shorter songs were tight, the longer, jammier songs were loose, and every gig was crammed full of plenty of each (it was a rare show that wrapped up before the three-hour mark). The only thing missing was Pig, back home in California, ostensibly to rest and recover, but in actuality never to return to the band or the stage. Pigpen may have been left behind, but judging by the acid-shattered look on Garcia's and Lesh's faces by about the halfway point of the show (the concert was recorded by a couple of young filmmakers and eventually released forty-one years later), it appears as if they brought a piece of San Francisco with them to Oregon in the form of plenty of good-quality Bay Area LSD. Probably in deference to the blazing heat (at one point Weir announces that they're going to change their name to the Sunstroke Serenaders), the band played three shorter sets instead of their customary two long ones. The opening set is very good (and very energetic, in spite of the temperature) but, aside from a smoking "China Cat Sunflower" > "I Know You Rider," not in the same league as its two successors. Not that the naked and half-naked people dancing, hugging, laughing, and passing the pipe were likely to have noticed. It's summertime and there's grass and trees and plenty of blue Oregon sky, so so what if we're running out of clean drinking water?—it's the Dead.

Things get going again with a textbook post-Europe "Playing in the Band" that's slippery smooth to begin *and* end with, and intricately involved in the middle, a perennial and perennially pleasing Grateful Dead paradox. "He's Gone" is goosebumpy and just starting to sprout the long, neo-gospel, Donna-abetted vocal outro that would make it even more moving as '72 turned into '73. "Jack Straw" is another great, newish song, sung and played with gusto and grace, but "Bird Song" is transcendent, Garcia at one point looking like even he's slightly surprised at the continuously weaving magic that he and Weir manage to create, Keith's piano here and elsewhere a tinkling, twinkling treat. There's not much professionally shot footage of the Dead during their peak performing period, so *Sunshine Daydream*, as the film was dubbed, is obligatory viewing, particularly for the close-ups of Garcia's never-idle fingers and the obliging eye contact shared between the band members. If only the film-makers had shown more of this, and fewer close-ups of tits and asses and cocks, and ditched the juvenile, pseudo-psychedelic animation that periodically—and frustratingly—supersedes such extremely rare concert footage.

"Dark Star" is a monster. It's psychedelic, it's jazz, it's full of all sorts of rich, creamy themes that are explored at lengthy leisure before being gently discarded for other promising astral avenues. The sun is beginning to set just as the opening four-note twin tingle of Lesh's bass and Garcia's guitar announce "Dark Star"'s arrival, and as the band play on and on (and *on*— at one point, Weir has clearly had it, he simply stops playing and hangs his hands at his sides before eventually taking a deep breath and diving back into the bubbling cosmic soup), and as the sun sinks lower and the sky darkens, and a couple of oblivious four- or five-year-olds scurry across the stage, it's almost too much. (How intense is it? After about thirty-one exhilarating minutes, when Weir *insists* that they wrap it up and the band clod-hops into "El Paso," it's actually a relief. Garcia, clearly stoned out of his mind and never playing better, sounds as if he wanted to slide into "Morning Dew" instead. When you're actually relieved that it's "El Paso" and not "Morning Dew," *that's* intense.)

And oh, yeah: with the Dead's help, the Springfield Cream-ery survived their economic downturn and managed to stay in business. In fact, they're still around today, albeit under a different name (Nancy's Yogurt). And nobody had to choose the least-deplorable candidate on the ballot or wear a button proclaiming that their candidate was best.

10/17/72 – *Fox Theatre, St Louis,* MO

1: Promised Land; Bird Song; El Paso; Sugaree; Me and My Uncle; Tennessee Jed; Big River; China Cat Sunflower>I Know You Rider; Black-Throated Wind; Deal; Cumberland Blues; Playing in the Band; Casey Jones

2: Greatest Story Ever Told; Don't Ease Me In; Mexicali Blues; Black Peter; Me and Bobby McGee; Bertha; Jack Straw; Friend of the Devil; Beat It On Down the Line; Ramble On Rose; Mississippi Half-Step Uptown Toodeloo>Sugar Magnolia>Not Fade Away>Going Down the Road Feeling Bad>Not Fade Away

E1: Uncle John's Band

E2: Johnny B. Goode

I'M AS GUILTY as anyone. When thoughts turn to the Dead and 1972, I immediately think of two things: Europe and Veneta. And why not? Every one of the twenty-two shows the group performed during their five weeks abroad is a keeper, a model of the "mature" Grateful Dead concert: plenty of first-rate shorter songs (many of them newly minted) in the first set, along with lots of longer jamming vehicles in the second, all of them played with energy, enthusiasm, and invention. Consistency and excellence rarely go hand in hand, but Europe '72 is an exception. Pick a show, pick any show, and just slip on your headphones and slide into aural ecstasy. And how can anyone overlook Veneta? A special time, a special day, a special show. So the fall of 1972 gets short shrift, which is wrong. It's no exaggeration to say that, beginning with the European shows in the spring of '72, the Dead rode a wave of sustained brilliance for two and a half years, until the "retirement" shows in the fall of '74.

Since the confessional is open, I might as well admit that I'm also culpable of a pronounced Space Head bias and generally prefer second sets to firsts. If, like me, your primary attraction to the Grateful Dead is Garcia's guitar, long jams are simply the most satisfactory way of experiencing his playing at its most adventurous, whether they turn out to be super spacey or not. But obviously there's a lot more to the Grateful Dead than that, and this show, the first of three consecutive nights at St Louis' funky little Fox Theatre, is proof. Two very notable exceptions aside (both occurring in the opening set), this show is all about the songs; lots and lots of them, and each one played and sung with palpable glee and grit. What's unique about it is that the songs never stop—there's no big second-set jamming or space vehicle, just more and more passionately performed songs. And you know what? That's okay. More than okay.

Any time the second tune of the night is a fifteen-minute "Bird Song," you know something is up (including the band's energy level). And this one isn't just protracted, it's mesmer-izing, Garcia and Weir and Lesh and Keith each contributing to a swirling kaleidoscope of sound that never eases up. (It's tunes like this that confirm what an utterly unique rhythm guitar player Weir had become. His plucks and strums and plunks and—just as important—breathy pauses are almost as compellingly singular as anything in either Garcia or Lesh's bag of stylistic ticks and tricks.) But there I go again: another hymn to another astonishing jam. It's a fourteen-song, hour-

and-a-half-plus first set, and the majority of the highlights are songy and never samey and frequently stunning. "Sugaree" is mid-tempo dreamy, "Me and My Uncle" scurries and smokes, "China Cat Sunflower">"I Know You Rider" jingle jangles in the proud midnight Missouri sun, "Black-Throated Wind" shows what Weir can do with a meaty ballad, "Cumberland Blues" tips its cowboy hat in the direction of the band's neo–country-and-western era, and "Casey Jones" is a good one, starting off, as usual, a mite leisurely, but building toward a thunderous, charging outro where Weir is in danger of shredding his voice before the second set even begins. As for the night's only extended-jamming vehicle, "Playing in the Band", it's conspicuous not only for its rarity, but for its quality. There's so much inventive, charging drama here in its mere twenty-four minutes, it dwarfs other, longer, more celebrated "Playing"s (the forty-six-minute 5/21/74 version, for example).

The second set is an anomaly: no marathon workouts like "Dark Star" or "The Other One," no extended jamming, no deep-space voyages. What it does have is another nearly hour-and-a-half-long smorgasbord of songs. Whether asymmetrical rockers ("Greatest Story Ever Told") or stoner country ("Ramble On Rose") or pumped-up polka ("Mexicali Blues") or neo-bluegrass ("Friend of the Devil") or dark dirges ("Black Peter"), it's all hard and sharp and clean and clear and pulsing with oomph and alacrity. It's impossible to gripe about the lack of lengthier pieces because there's simply no time to complain, the tunes just keep coming and coming. The five-song medley that wraps things up is a corker, all right ("Mississippi Half-Step Uptown Toodeloo," in only its eighteenth performance, already gets the goosebumps going by song's end, and if "Sugar Magnolia">"Not Fade Away">"Going Down the Road Feeling Bad">"Not Fade Away" don't *compel* you to your feet, it's time to take up tiddlywinks), but the band never takes it outside, just keeps the pedal to the metal and blasts away with both barrels until concert's end.

Incredibly, after so much music already (nearly three-and-a-half high-octane hours), the Dead even manage not one but two encores. And this was only the first show.

10/18/72 – *Fox Theatre, St Louis,* MO

1: Bertha; Me and My Uncle; Don't Ease Me In; Mexicali Blues; Brown-Eyed Women; Beat It On Down the Line; Bird Song; Big River; Loser; Jack Straw; Big Railroad Blues; El Paso; China Cat Sunflower>I Know You Rider

2: Playing in the Band>Drums>Dark Star>Morning Dew>Playing in the Band; Deal; Promised Land; Brokedown Palace; One More Saturday Night; Casey Jones

NATURALLY, THE NEXT night it's all about "Dark Star." Which helps to explain why otherwise sane people need to hear every note of every Grateful Dead concert: because you don't know what will happen. Not only do you not know what they'll play, you don't know how they'll play it. In a world of stultifying—and increasing—homogeneity (artistic and otherwise), the Dead, at their best, resist predictability and conventionality. *Thrive on it,* in fact. October 18, 1972, for example, the band's second night of three at the same cozy St Louis venue, might be just another stop on just another Midwestern tour, featuring all of the familiar hallmarks of a great Grateful Dead show, but it also includes that extra-special something that makes it more than a little memorable. *10/18/72* memorable.

A mere glance at the set list instantly indicates where the major magic occurs, and "Playing in the Band">"Drums">"Dark Star">"Morning Dew">"Playing in the Band" doesn't disappoint (how could it?), but the opening set shouldn't be overlooked. It's another long set, for one thing (fourteen songs and seventy-nine minutes), and bing bang boom, the Dead race from one success to the next, the usual unusual mix of rockers, ballads, folk-rock, country songs, and a memento from their old jug-band days exhibiting the full range of the Dead's characteristic genre hopping. The second "Bird Song" in as many nights is a spacey appetizer to the far-out four-course meal to come, an uncommon combination of a beautiful song and virtuoso jamming (at 13:06, it's also the lengthiest song of the opening set). "Loser" is typically spine-tingling, and Garcia's clearly having a ball tearing off twangy leads on Weir's trio of cowboy songs, but "China Cat Sunflower" > "I Know You Rider" is when the Dead shift into another gear entirely.

The last sequence of the set, it glows and glides and gradually builds in power until it feels like the onset of a good THC high. Sounds acquire colour, individual instruments meld in all sorts of illuminating ways (the interaction between Weir's spider-web-weaving rhythm guitar and Garcia's delicate-but-driving lead is especially elating), previously unutilized crevices in your cranium burst with novel connections and questions and insights. And some of the gentle jamming that occurs early in the segue is astonishingly beautiful. As good as it is, though, it's just a tingling tease of the full-blown brain blast to come. And it begins with the opening number of the second set.

Actually, it precedes that. Before the familiar circular chords of "Playing in the Band" commence, the band can he heard nervously joking around about the quartet of tunes they've just this instant decided to link together. Garcia jokes, "Hold on tight," Lesh laughs, and Weir counts it off. To keep things interesting, the Dead would sometimes split up songs (e.g., "Dark Star" > "El Paso" > "Dark Star"), but this was the first time they spliced "Playing in the Band" together with another tune or tunes, something they wouldn't do again until 10/21/73.

"Playing" had expanded and intensified during the European shows, as Dead tunes sometimes did, and was now routinely clocking in at twenty minutes or more, the majority of it dedicated to deep space travel. This one is no different. Everyone shines, including Kreutzmann, but it's worth considering how his light touch and unremitting fills and dependable cymbal crashes during the long voyage out are all timely and tasty, yet sometimes he still exhibits difficulty in simply keeping the beat on much-more-straightforward tunes. (It doesn't help that Lesh is usually content to leave the more-mundane aspects of timekeeping to the drummer or drummers.) If Miles Davis was correct when he claimed that the Dead were a jazz band who played rock and roll, then Kreutzmann was a jazz drummer who played rock and roll, which could cut both ways.

The "Dark Star" that follows has got it all—jamming, space, lots of spook—but what stands out most (the stunning stuff that Garcia gets up to at around the fourteen-minute mark excepted) are the rumbling bass bombs Lesh unloads near its completion, a stunning solo display of garage-rock be-bop that leaves the band nowhere else to go but on to the next tune. The transition into "Morning Dew" is a little rough, but the tune itself is anything but, is a silky slice of post-apocalyptic sorrow that's the worldly yin to "Dark Star"'s otherworldly yang. Then it's back into "Playing in the Band" for five and a half more delicious minutes, at the conclusion of which the Dead have been playing non-stop for over an hour.

They manage to crank out a few more tunes, including a sweetly sorrowful "Brokedown Palace," two frisky rockers, and a slow-building "Uncle John's Band," but it hardly matters. Most of us are still floating around somewhere in the galaxy. Thanks for the ride. Let's do it again tomorrow night.

6/10/73 – *Robert F. Kennedy Memorial Stadium, Washington, DC*

1: Morning Dew; Beat It On Down the Line; Ramble On Rose; Jack Straw; Wave That Flag; Looks Like Rain; Box of Rain; They Love Each Other; The Race Is On; Row Jimmy; El Paso; Bird Song; Playing in the Band

2: Eyes of the World > Stella Blue; Big River; Here Comes Sunshine; Around and Around; Dark Star > He's Gone > Wharf Rat > Truckin'; Sugar Magnolia

3: It Takes a Lot to Laugh, It Takes a Train to Cry; That's All Right, Mama; Promised Land; Not Fade Away > Going Down the Road Feeling Bad > Drums > Not Fade Away; Johnny B. Goode

NOT GIVING A shit counts. Not doing what you're supposed to do just because you're supposed to do it is a virtue. And sometimes the best way to illustrate your indifference to the blessed twin sanctities of popular esteem and economic security that come with being a bonafide big-time success is to *actively* not give a shit. When the Grateful Dead made their first foray to Europe in the spring of 1970—shortly before the release of the almost-radio-friendly *Workingman's Dead* and their delighted record label's decision to spend a few bucks and get their potential hit-makers (Ha!) a little trans-Atlantic publicity—they were clearly on the reluctant road to rock-star glory. Rock hadn't yet entirely ossified into just another branch plant (Entertainment Division) of American Big Business, but the Moloch that is mainstream America already had its slithery, shiny manacles wrapped tight around the neck of what was once intended to be—for bands like the Dead, anyway—that most irrelevant of societal activities: art.

Big houses and multiple cars and private jets had become customary for rock-and-roll royalty by the turn of the decade, and if the Grateful Dead played their cards right, there was no reason why they couldn't get in on the action, too. So what did the Dead do? They dosed the camera crew that had been assigned by Warner Brothers to record their showcase gig for future promotional use, thereby rendering much of the resultant footage all but useless. Why? Because turning straight people on to psychedelics was a higher priority than looking cool on camera and furthering their career. Need another reason? It might be *fun*, the best reason to do anything.

Refusing to break a sweat for anything as ignoble as popularity or prosperity is one thing, but allowing some other band to blow you off the stage was sufficient grounds to get serious. When the Grateful Dead and the Allman Brothers Band agreed to co-bill back-to-back nights at cavernous RFK Memorial Stadium in early June, 1973, the Allmans were at the height of their popularity (an AM-radio hit single like "Ramblin' Man" will do that) and likely the main reason the promoters believed they could fill a one-hundred-thousand-seat football stadium. (Multi-group festivals aside, this was the Dead's first real mega-gig, although they and the Allman Brothers, plus the Band, would perform before a record-breaking six hundred thousand people, a portion of whom actually bought tickets, six weeks later at Watkins Glen, New York.) The bands took turns opening and closing, with the Dead acting as the Allmans' opening act the first night before trading places the next.

The Saturday show is great—it's the Dead, it's '73, how could it be otherwise?—but their closing show on the tenth is preternaturally great. Naturally. This was important. This was about the music. "Foremost we admire the outlaw with the strength of his convictions," the poet Robert Duncan wrote. On June 10, 1973, the Dead—the cosmic clown jesters of contemporary music—weren't messing around.

Opening up with "Morning Dew" is the first and best indication that the band obviously considered this a special show, requiring special songs and special playing. An eleven-minute, post-apocalyptic dirge is not your customary rock-and-roll-show kickoff (especially after a couple hours of boogie-till-you-puke blues rock), but it certainly would have caught the massive audience's attention, which was probably the point. Also, since Washington, DC, is where, quite possibly, the decision will be made to push the button that launches the missiles that relegate *homo sapiens* to the history books, why not begin the proceedings with a paean to homegrown, nuclear-powered human stupidity and sorrow? And then immediately follow it up with a jaunty little old jug-band tune like "Beat It On Down the Line" about, among other things, rushing home from work to get some nice homemade nooky? Tonight, the Dead could do it all—and they did. *All* of it.

New songs (in-progress material like "Here Comes Sunshine" and "Row Jimmy" and an off-key "Stella Blue" that would end up on their next album, *Wake of the Flood*). Relatively recent classics, none more than two years old ("Ramble On Rose" and "Jack Straw"). Familiar favourites ("Morning Dew" and "Beat It On Down the Line"). Country ("Big River" and "The Race Is On"). Rock and roll ("Around and Around"). Rarities (the fourth-to-last "Box of Rain" to be played for thirteen years). And because they were the Dead, songs that weren't even songs yet (the last performance of "Wave That Flag," the slightly cluttered prototype of "us Blues"). And those are just the toe-tappers.

Because of the occasion, the quality of the first-set jams (a gorgeous "Bird Song" and an exceptionally spacey "Playing in the Band") can go toe-to-toe with most shows' big second-set highlights. When they finally do make it to the second set after a very long first (thirteen songs over nearly ninety minutes), "Dark Star" > "He's Gone" > "Wharf Rat" > "Truckin'" is all that needs to be said: almost an hour of ceaseless, churning brilliance of all types and tones. Oh, and the set-opening "Eyes of the World" might be the most exciting thing performed all night, Garcia a jazzy dream weaver on lead guitar, and Lesh and Keith gleefully counterpointing back and forth, back and forth, and sounding nearly as compelling.

And the encore? Special night, special encore: "It Takes a Lot to Laugh, It Takes a Train to Cry," "That's All Right, Mama," "Promised Land," "Not Fade Away" > "Going Down the Road Feeling Bad" > "Drums" > "Not Fade Away," "Johnny B. Goode." A couple members of the Allman Brothers join the Dead for this unofficial third set, and although it's a big boisterous mess (if very enjoyable for this very reason), Garcia still manages to dazzle with some blistering leads on "That's All Right, Mama" and "Going Down the Road Feeling Bad." Sometimes giving a shit can be a lot of fun too.

9/7/73 – *Nassau Veterans Memorial Coliseum, Uniondale*, NY

1: Promised Land; Sugaree; Mexicali Blues; They Love Each Other; Jack Straw; Looks Like Rain; Deal; El Paso; Bird Song; Playing in the Band

2: Here Comes Sunshine; Me and My Uncle; Loser; Let It Grow > Stella Blue; Truckin' > Drums > The Other One > Eyes of the World > Sugar Magnolia

E: Around and Around

HOCKEY RINKS AREN'T for hearing music. Not music you're supposed to *listen* to. And not just because, for instance, the Nassau Veterans Memorial Coliseum, home of the NHL's New York Islanders, is your archetypal late-twentieth-century, all-purpose, suburban concrete shitbox; but because a crowd of fourteen thousand concertgoers staring up at six specks on stage is not an environment particularly conducive to fostering genuine creative symbiosis. (We're here! We're high! Entertain us!) But this is where the Grateful Dead found themselves for two consecutive nights in early September 1973, their growing popularity necessitating bigger and bigger venues, the increasing cost of carrying on as a keep-on-truckin'-on business entity dictating that they generate more and more income. And since their records never really sold—even the albums that were, by their own modest standards, relatively successful, never approached the sales figures of the era's big rock-and-roll acts—that meant steady touring.

The best they could do in such less-than-ideal circumstances, it seemed, was to make the concert experience as enjoyable as possible for everyone, namely by undertaking the creation of the largest, loudest, most expensive in-concert sound system ever created. Which, naturally, meant more hard slogging on the concrete-cavern circuit to accumulate the cash needed to make their auditory ambitions a reality. Just a quick question, though, before the curtain comes up: how did we end up as businessmen? When exactly did this become a job?

Admittedly, fourteen thousand people cheering and clapping and stomping along has to have its appeal, and every song in the first set pulses with a palpable energy, although that may have owed as much to this being the Dead's first live gig in five weeks as to the large, enthusiastic crowd. The group had been busy recording their album *Wake of the Flood*, the first for their new, band-owned-and-operated record label, another attempt to exist as independently as possible within the cramped confines of the music industry.

By 1972 the Dead and their management and the coterie of true believers who made up the extended Grateful Dead family were determined to leave Warner Brothers when their contract expired and be their own record label. A handful of other rock-and-roll bands had attempted something similarly bold—the Beatles and the Rolling Stones and even fellow San Franciscans Jefferson Airplane—but in each case the actual records were distributed by a conglomerate (Capitol, Atlantic, and RCA, respectively), meaning that a lot of the day-to-day business details and duties were handled by someone else. Not the Dead. The Dead were all in. The reasons why the band wanted to be their own corporate overseers were various. There was the subpar material quality of the actual records themselves. There was a perceived lack of promotional efficiency on the part of Warner Brothers. There was their shrunken slice of the royalty pie. There was the simple incongruity of a bunch of stoned, merrymaking beatniks partnering up with a suit-and-tied megacorporation. Not even Pigpen's sadly inevitable death, six months before, could slow down the Good Ship Grateful.

The five weeks off the road, while tending to business and making *Wake of the Flood*, would help explain a certain sloppiness and occasional off-key singing and missed instrumental cues throughout the show. There's a certain sloppiness and occasional off-key singing and missed instrumental cues during pretty much *every* Grateful Dead concert, but this one has a few more. On the whole, it's a spirited if unspectacular first set. Until the last two songs before the break.

"Bird Song" features plenty of shimmering Fender Rhodes from Keith, sounding at times like cosmic-jazz keyboardist Lonnie Liston Smith; fused with the winding gyre of Garcia's guitar, it's where the show takes off, and it never comes down until "Around and Around"'s final frantic notes. "Playing in the Band" (a first-set closer) is a mere 17:55, a tidy, tranquil tornado—even when Garcia's using the wah-wah—the deep, mellow jamming and intense interplay between Garcia, Lesh, Weir, and Keith what this version of "Playing" is all about. Its concentrated concision is what makes it a standout.

Although *Wake of the Flood* wouldn't be released until mid-November, over the next two nights the group would play every cut off the upcoming LP, including 9/7/73's second-set opener "Here Comes Sunshine," in all of its broken–music box charm; "Let It Grow," in its live debut (sans Donna's harmony vocals, which hadn't been worked out yet, and thereby deprived of a portion of its power); and an aching "Stella Blue" (a tenderly tinkling Keith simply triumphant throughout). "Stella Blue" wasn't the first time Hunter employed the image of life as a dream (the words he wrote for Lesh's "Box of Rain" being another), but it's not Buddhist dogma he evokes, so much as Shakespeare's *Tempest*, when Prospero says, "We are such stuff as dreams are made on, and our little life is rounded with a sleep." "Stella Blue" *is* like life: evanescent, sad, beautiful. But the highlight of the second set is what *doesn't* get played.

After a well-received "Truckin'" (this and "Casey Jones" were, after all, two of the main radio reasons why so many new fans flocked to their shows) and a brief snatch of "Drums," it's a pulsating "The Other One" (in spite of a flubbed opening) that features lots of Garcia's snaking, snarling lead guitar. Lots, that is, until the 7:10 mark—deep in the deep of a lovely spacey lull periodically punctuated by some forbidding bass-guitar belches courtesy of Lesh—that's it for this one, Garcia can't wait any longer, he simply *has* to strum the opening chords to "Eyes of the World," another just-recorded tune. Ironically, considering it would eventually lose much of its breezy, samba-like charm (another late-'70s cocaine casualty of rushed rhythms and over-busy drumming, perhaps), this one starts off sluggish but eventually rights itself and just...cooks. It's longer than the average "Eyes" (19:02), and you only wish it was longer, that it would go on forever, wave after wave of jubilant Garcia guitar notes fluttering, floating, filling the nose-bleed section of the Islanders' home arena. If you listen to the show, you can still hear them.

10/30/73 – *Kiel Auditorium, St Louis,* MO

1: Here Comes Sunshine; Me and My Uncle; Ramble On Rose; Looks Like Rain; Deal; Mexicali Blues; They Love Each Other; El Paso; Row Jimmy; Jack Straw; China Cat Sunflower>I Know You Rider; Playing in the Band

2: Mississippi Half-Step Uptown Toodeloo; Big River; Dark Star>Stella Blue>Eyes of the World>Weather Report Suite (i. Prelude; ii. Part One; iii. Let It Grow); Going Down the Road Feeling Bad>Johnny B. Goode

E: One More Saturday Night

CRUISE CONTROL DOESN'T have to mean snooze control, just like comfortable need not imply complacent. The Grateful Dead might have been able to waltz into St Louis and *la de da* play a couple of stunning shows with almost zero song overlap (a few tunes off their just-released LP excepted), but it was a proficiency born of near-constant, high-level, high-wire playing, not hardened habit. And they weren't just busy touring.

Determined to cut out the corporate middleman and be rock-and-roll Don Quixotes, the band had released their latest album, *Wake of the Flood*, only two weeks previously, the first for their very own Grateful Dead Records. Massive amounts of energy and money were being channeled into the development of what would become the Wall of Sound, a state-of-the-art sound system that would make even the most echo-laden hockey rink acoustically acceptable. And if all that weren't enough, Garcia, as usual, was using what little downtime the Dead did have to busily pursue not one but *two* side projects:

his nameless, funky bar band with Merl Saunders; and Old
& In the Way, the bluegrass group he co-founded with David
Grisman and Peter Rowan.

In the midst of the fall 1973 Grateful Dead tour, which totaled
thirty-nine shows from the first week of September until the
middle of December, one finds, for example, the Dead playing
a characteristically spectacular gig at Northwestern University
in Evanston, Illinois, on November 1; Garcia performing two
days later with Sanders et al. at the Keystone in Berkeley, California; right back at it the next night with Old & In the Way
at Sonoma State University in Rohnert Park, California; and
hooking up with Saunders again at the Keystone the night after
that; followed by three consecutive evenings with the Grateful Dead, back home in San Francisco, at Winterland, from
November 9 to 11. In January, Garcia would begin recording
his second solo LP, this time for the boutique record label the
band created for solo projects and less commercially viable
projects, Round Records.

Artists, if they're talented enough and hard-working enough
and lucky enough, discover their own voices at some point.
If and when they do, they're cooking with gas; all they need
is a match to light the fire and get the party started. When
you no longer spend your time finding out who you are, you
can spend it instead *being* who you are. By 1973, for better or
for worse (both come with having your own style), the Dead
were the Dead. And on October 30, 1973, the Grateful Dead
were in St Louis, Missouri, to play the 9,300-seat Kiel Auditorium, having already turned in a typical socko performance
the night before at the same venue. (Unfortunately, their increasing popularity meant that the Fox Theatre, where they'd
played three times in '72, was simply too small now.) As al-

ready noted, from 1972 to 1974 the live Dead could do no wrong, so just a glance at the set list from the previous night's gig is sufficient testament to how good the show was. (If the "Eyes of the World" > "China Doll" doesn't do it for you, the "Truckin'" > "The Other One" > "Wharf Rat" > "Sugar Magnolia" will.) The next night was even better.

The major musical statements might have been reserved for the show's second half, but any set that concludes with "China Cat Sunflower" > "I Know You Rider" and "Playing in the Band" shouldn't be overlooked (even if, in good ol' Grateful Dead fashion, the former is rocky rhythmically and Weir messes up the words to the latter). As wonderful as the music that the band made during their peak period is, it's not one extended, stylistically undifferentiated era. Not only did the Dead's sound get progressively jazzier overall, but each year has its own flavor, and '73 shows tend to be gentler and more introspective. This is reflected not only in some of the songs Garcia and Weir were coming up with at this time (e.g., Garcia's show-opening "Here Comes Sunshine" and the first two, pastoral-pretty sections of Weir's "Weather Report Suite"), but also in the way older songs sometimes metamorphosed into intriguingly mellower versions of their former selves. The "Dark Star" that comes early in the second set here is one of these, a dripping, almost lullaby-like excursion into the ether that even includes Garcia laying down some laid-back slide guitar. What it possibly lacks in agreeable throb and teeth-rattling, celestial cacophony, it makes up for in silky, stargazing aplomb. It may not go anywhere in particular, but the view from space is consistently inspiring nonetheless. (And the bass bombs Lesh periodically sets off are there to make sure you don't get *too* cosmically comfortable.)

The transition from a twenty-eight-minute "Dark Star" into a gently bruised "Stella Blue" is so seamless it can only be described as *inevitable*. Thematically, the pairing is also ideal, the beautiful nothingness of space redeemed by the enduring import of nothing more than a song or a line of lyric or even an almost-forgotten melody—music, emancipating music, the answer to eternity's enormous *Why*? After nearly forty minutes, even the staunchest Space Head is probably beginning to grow a little oxygen- and sunshine-deprived, so Garcia concludes "Stella Blue" by immediately strumming the exultant introductory chords to "Eyes of the World," Garcia and Lesh, the two soloists, so attuned to each other throughout that at times it sounds like someone playing both instruments simultaneously.

Having performed continuously—and brilliantly—for nearly an hour by now, this should be enough. And it might have been, some other time, but tonight the Dead surge into the stark guitar introduction to a nearly sixteen-minute "Weather Report Suite," another number off the new album. Damn, if they don't make that seem easy, too.

12/19/73 – *Curtis Hixon Convention Hall, Tampa,* FL

1: Promised Land; Sugaree; Mexicali Blues; Dire Wolf;
Black-Throated Wind; Candy Man; Jack Straw; Big
Railroad Blues; Big River; Here Comes Sunshine; El Paso;
Ramble On Rose; Playing in the Band

2: Mississippi Half-Step Uptown Toodeloo; Me
and Bobby McGee; Row Jimmy; Weather Report
Suite (i. Prelude; ii. Part One; iii. Let It Grow); He's
Gone > Truckin' > Nobody's Fault But Mine > The Other
One > Stella Blue; Around and Around

E: Casey Jones

OBVIOUSLY, THERE'S NO such thing as a perfect or greatest
Grateful Dead concert—how could there be? If what you're
craving is psychedelic-suffused space rock, you're probably
going to search out a Dead show from 1968–69; on the other
hand, if what you mostly feel like doing is singing along to
some really good, catchy tunes, chances are it'll be one of the
acoustic sets the band played in 1970 or a fiery first set from
1972 full of newly-written toe-tappers that you'll find yourself
listening to. And why would anyone want to choose between
the two? Why would you want to privilege one kind of musical
experience over another or even limit yourself to only one kind
of experience? A fork can be a very useful utensil, but it's not
much use when you're eating soup.

   Still, every Head has their favourite Grateful Dead era or
eras and shows, which is as it should be; as Popeye so sensibly
reminds us, *I yam what I yam.* I'm an aficionado of 1971–74

Dead, and have yet to hear a concert recorded during this period that didn't titillate and astound. Garcia, Lesh, and Keith
never played with more facility and gusto, a peak performing
period for all three (and Weir was right there too, adding his
distinctive rhythm-guitar parts whenever necessary, as well as
not playing anything when it wasn't). Donna wasn't entirely
integrated into the band's music yet (meaning she didn't sing
on many of the songs that predated her and Keith's joining up),
but was an integral part of most of the newer tunes, providing
the music with bracing vocal harmonies unimagined before
her arrival. Speaking of which, there was such an abundance of
dazzling originals by this time, in such a staggering number of
styles and tones, that every set list is a smorgasbord of sound.
A Dead show during this era is like what they say about the
weather in Kansas: if you don't like it, just wait a few minutes.

But maybe what makes this three-year interval so compelling,
most of all, is the jazzy direction the band had taken. (And not
just on the newer material—e.g., "Eyes of the World"—that
so easily opened up to the fiery finesse of Garcia's lead guitar
and Lesh's adventurous bass and Keith's nimble-fingered piano
playing, but which also suffused so much of their older music—e.g., "Playing in the Band.") This was a group of musicians
that *listened* to what each other was playing. The whole is greater than the already-great parts because the parts were paying
attention to—and frequently being inspired by—the other
parts. That's jazz. And 12/19/73 is the Dead at their jazzy best.

This isn't tasteful fusion music, either—these are *songs* that
are jazzy-jammed out, songs with memorable melodies and
solid structures and evocative lyrics. Which only makes them
all the more impactful when the jazzy fireworks do get lit. The
first nine numbers are typical first-set material, if enthusiasti-

cally performed and thoroughly enjoyable, but by the time of the tenth, the mid-tempo mellowed brilliance of "Here Comes Sunshine," everything ascends to another level—the locked-in rhythm, the instrumental interplay, the group vocals. Even though it's only the first set, Garcia takes scintillating solo after solo, the others faithfully following along and adding their own respective top-shelf touches as he picks and strums his way to six-string heaven. When Garcia is on, as he obviously is tonight, even upbeat fun filler like "Big River" burns, becomes shit-kicking cosmic country you'd be happy to put up your feet and listen to all night. A powerfully protean "Playing in the Band" is a big sloppy bowl of hot sound soup whose main ingredients—Garcia's wailing wah-wah, Keith's mischievous right hand, Lesh's restless bass, Weir's airy, spare rhythm guitar, and Kreutzmann's tasteful fills—are left to simmer for twenty-one delicious minutes. And that's just the first set.

Second-set opener "Mississippi Half-Step Uptown Toodeloo" contains plenty of Garcia's squiggly guitar genius, but what makes it such an overall success is Kreutzmann's light touch on the drums, almost as if he's playing *on top of* the other instruments instead of underneath. Weir's "Weather Report Suite" is worth it just to hear Garcia play slide guitar (unlike most guitar players who pick up a bottleneck, he still sounds like himself and not like just another standard slide player jamming the blooze). And while I'd never claim that 12/19/73 is the single best Grateful Dead show ever (how could I, when only the night before and at the same venue: "Weather Report Suite (i. Prelude; ii. Part One; iii. Let It Grow)" > "Dark Star" > "Drums" > "Eyes of the World" > "Wharf Rat" > "Sugar Magnolia"?), it is my go-to concert—that is, whenever I feel the need to proselytize, I stop talking and simply play this show's glorious guts, the quintet of interconnected tunes in the middle of the second set. What a staggering succession of brilliance.

"He's Gone" manages to be both tenderly poignant and aptly insolent, and the neo-gospel outro could never go on too long. "Truckin'" is what it is: Google Maps for the metaphysically inclined life traveller. "Nobody's Fault But Mine" is Garcia's best-ever blues shot, his guitar doing all the real talking, although his brief, matter-of-fact vocals are full of legitimate sorrow and honest self-recrimination. "The Other One" is long, passionate, and pulverizing. And the jams that bisect it are bonkers (the first very jazzy jammy; the second sci-fi skronky and bass-bomb scary). *Bonkers*. "Stella Blue" (featuring some exquisite soloing) is what it all means: in the end, after everything else, all there is, is song.

The only thing missing is Donna's vocals (pregnant with her and Keith's child, she's absent during the entire concert), particularly on closer "Around and Around," where Weir's histrionic screams can't compensate for Donna's joyful wails). But that's okay. No show's perfect.

3/23/74 – *Cow Palace, Daly City,* CA

1: US Blues; Promised Land; Brown-Eyed Women; Mexicali Blues; Tennessee Jed; Black-Throated Wind; Scarlet Begonias; Beat It On Down the Line; It Must Have Been the Roses; El Paso; Deal; Cassidy; China Cat Sunflower>I Know You Rider; Weather Report Suite (i. Prelude; ii. Part One; iii. Let It Grow)

2: Playing in the Band>Uncle John's Band>Morning Dew>Uncle John's Band>Playing in the Band; Ship of Fools; Big River; Ramble On Rose; Me and My Uncle; Bertha; Around and Around; Wharf Rat>Sugar Magnolia; Casey Jones

E: One More Saturday Night

HERE'S HOW WE got here: because of their growing popularity, the Grateful Dead felt obligated to play larger and larger venues. Because they were playing larger and larger venues, they also felt compelled to design and build a better sound system than was commercially available, if they wanted all the people at the back of the hockey rinks and outdoor stadiums to hear more than vaguely familiar clamour and clatter. So they commissioned their technical team to create the best sound system possible, the Wall of Sound. Which, not surprisingly, turned out also to be the most expensive sound system possible. (About a million and a half dollars in contemporary currency, and at a time when the band members were living on a stipend of a few hundred dollars a week. Talk about putting your money where your mouth is.) Which meant playing even more, even bigger gigs to pay for six hundred speakers and twenty-six thousand watts of power and a dozen roadies to put it together and take it apart and get it to the next hockey rink on time so they could do it all over again. But that's later. Right now, it's March 23, 1974, the official "sound test" of the Wall of Sound.

And what better way to inaugurate a new era in Grateful Dead history than with only the third performance of "US Blues," a state-of-the-union rocker that has some nifty chord changes and chugs along just fine and contains some of Hunter's cleverest, most caustic lyrics. And what could be more Dead—what could be more like life?—than their state-of-the-art, astronomically expensive sound system immediately screwing up and Garcia's guitar going missing during the opening song of the night? The crew eventually figures it out, though, and a long first set ensues, which includes not only the third-ever "It Must Have Been the Roses," but the debuts of "Scarlet Begonias" and "Cassidy."

"Roses" is a rarity—a solely Hunter-written composition per-formed by the Dead—and is sad and pretty and an ideal ballad vehicle for Garcia, with as much room for his emotive lead guitar as for his voice. As might be expected, "Scarlet" sounds uncer-tain in places and a little slow, but its bouncy charm is obvious. (Although without Donna's vocals, which had yet to be worked out, it sounds a tad emaciated.) "Cassidy" isn't a new song—it originally appeared on Weir's first solo album, 1972's *Ace*—and wouldn't be played live again until 1976, but it's one of those melodically skewed tunes that Weir did so well and that pro-vide such an effective counterpoint to Garcia's more traditional song structures. Garcia gets the words to "I Know You Rider" wrong, but it doesn't matter because the band is smokin', and why wouldn't they be? With speakers that reach as high as a three-storey house, even in as uninviting a concert venue as the Cow Palace (seating capacity thirteen thousand, and which regularly hosted not only rock concerts, but a variety of sporting events, roller derby, and actual livestock conventions and rodeos), the music is loud and clear and rich. Just as importantly, it was loud and clear and rich not just to the audience, but to the *band*, an indispensable ingredient if the goal is symbiotic playing.

On paper, the obvious highpoint of the evening is the "Playing in the Band" > "Uncle John's Band" > "Morning Dew" > "Uncle John's Band" > "Playing in the Band" sequence that opens the second set. It's impressive, no doubt, but some of the transitions are a trifle awkward (Wall of Sound jitters?), and there are better versions of this particular extended collection of tunes available (such as 11/17/73). It's what happens about a minute in that is particularly noteworthy, when Weir, whose vocals have been virtually undetectable, shuts "Playing" down with a frustrated "Wait a minute, wait a minute." The band stops playing, Lesh utters a couple of *Sorry*s, and while everyone plucks and plonks and tries to stays loose, the crew gets busy figuring out what's wrong. When Weir and the audience can finally hear him again, "A thousand pardons, folks, we'll try it one more time," he offers, and the Dead do, indeed, give it a second shot. Even the most-novice garage band knows that if something goes wrong on stage—speaker or microphone malfunction, a busted instrument, whatever—you're never supposed to stop playing. *Never*. What could be more unprofessional than to stop the show? And what could be more Dead—and less showbiz—than to do just that (and have the audience cheer when they do)?

The remainder of the concert is technologically glitch free, and the band plays on and on, like they can't get enough of their brand-new toy (an especially eerie "Wharf Rat" the best of the bunch). Three and a half hours later, the results of the sound test are in: The Wall of Sound passed. So did the Dead.

5/21/74 – *Hec Edmundson Pavilion, University of Washington, Seattle,* WA

1: Me and My Uncle; Brown-Eyed Women; Beat It On Down the Line; Deal; Mexicali Blues; It Must Have Been the Roses; The Race Is On; Scarlet Begonias; El Paso; Row Jimmy; Money Money; Ship of Fools; Weather Report Suite (i. Prelude; ii. Part One; iii. Let It Grow); China Doll

2: Playing in the Band; US Blues; Big River; Stella Blue; Around and Around; Eyes of the World; Wharf Rat > Sugar Magnolia

E: Johnny B. Goode

THEY CAME TO hear the band, they came to see the Wall of Sound, they got what they came for. Two months in, the reviews were rapturous: the new sound system was an oxymoron of aural delight, delicate thunder from six-hundred-plus speakers that dwarfed the musicians and ensured that every subtlety of sound was pumped into every amphitheatre or concrete block–arena crevice. And the music itself was pretty wonderful too. For some Heads, including this one, it doesn't get much better. How could it? Plenty of great songs, plenty of inspired jamming, plenty of deep space; a little superlative something of everything that the Dead so inimitably did so well. There was some concern that lugging around the Wall of Sound was costing the band far more money than they'd planned, and that the expanded road crew was averaging about four hours of sleep a night, just to ensure that the colossal sound system got there, got set up, got torn down, and got

back on the road again, but the Dead took pride in not sweat-
ing the small stuff until it became big stuff. And then ignoring
it once it did.

The first set does what it's supposed to do: gets both the
band and the audience humming. The standout track is probably "Row Jimmy," Garcia's slide guitar a welcome rarity, a
tender, crying timbre to be added to his growing arsenal of
electric-guitar goodies. Also noteworthy is Keith's Fender
Rhodes, which he manages to make sound like an organ on
this and a few other tunes. Piano was Keith's instrument of
choice, a refreshing acoustical undergrowth to the electrical
firestorm that so often blazed above it, but his use of Fender
Rhodes in '73 and '74 was a nice bright addition to the band's
sound and perfectly suited to much of the newer, jazzier
material. (Or, in the case of the velvety "Row Jimmy," refur-
bished reggae.) In only its tenth performance, "China Doll" is
a little brief, at 5:48, but already a chilling stunner. The key to
its spooky success doesn't lie in the lyrics or its subject matter
(a self-inflicted pistol shot), but in the musical arrangement,
all of the instruments seeming to hang suspended in mid-air
until Garcia's stirring solo, a floating fantasia that, once heard,
won't be forgotten.

The opening set also includes the third, and final, performance of Weir and Barlow's "Money Money." Grateful Dead
lore has it that the song was dropped because fans found it
sexist or even misogynistic, and maybe that is why. (There
aren't many artists who enjoy tormenting their audiences with
patently unpopular material.) But while it isn't anti-women—
it's about a specific *person*: money hungry and status seeking
and who uses sex to get next to a rich rock star, a very real type
of person—it is a pretty lousy song. Melodically unremarkable

and reliant on repetition to hold it together, it's just not good art. Which is the right reason not to listen to it.

If you mention 5/21/74 to most Heads, they'll probably answer with four words and an exclamation mark: "'Playing in the Band'!" That's because the version here that opens up the second set is the longest single song the Dead ever played, forty-seven minutes of non-stop action, over three-quarters of an hour of peak '74 Dead. What could go wrong? Nothing, really—except that there's also nothing really right about it either. Oh, they jam all right, and even approach deep space more than once, but not much takes hold, nothing develops into anything interesting until the thirty-six-minute mark, when Garcia gets ahold of a compelling collection of notes, but it's too late in the game to alter the end result. This is bad, this is good, this is as it should be. Large chunks of this leviathan are given over to skronky screeching and affectless noodling, the players never gaining a foothold in "Playing in the Band"'s normally fecund form (some of their career-best jams occur during "Playing"). It sounds like someone desperate to come and fucking and fucking and still not being able to reach orgasm. But this is only because the musical questing for something special is real, if futile. If it wasn't, it wouldn't feel so exasperating. Working without a net is exhilarating; it's also dangerous. And you can't have one without the other.

Give the Dead their due, though: only they would have had the courage or been so foolish as to open up with such a mammoth anticlimax. But with plenty of time left to go— this is the Grateful Dead circa the mid-1970s, after all, whose shows rarely wrapped up in less than three hours—there's ample opportunity to turn things round. Which, because this is the Grateful Dead circa the mid-1970s, they do, again and again. Lesh's bass on "Stella Blue" seems less like a musical instrument than a gently treading ghost. A frisky "Around and Around" suffers for being shut down too soon, but Keith beats the shit out of his piano enough to make it a rip-snortin' good time, anyway. (Who says he couldn't rock out when he felt like it?) At a mere 13:52, "Eyes of the World" contains all of the inspired jamming that "Playing in the Band" lacked, Lesh the soloing star tonight. "Wharf Rat" is lessened by Donna's absence—as with "Around and Around," she'd add her own parts to several of these older tunes over time—but it's still "Wharf Rat," as inviolable a song as exists in the Grateful Dead canon.

And when they slide into "Sugar Magnolia"—Garcia blasting out sunshine-daydream sunbeams from start to finish—it's time to be happy just to be alive. Which was something else the audience came for. And got.

9/10/74 – *Alexandra Palace, London, England*

1: Around and Around; Mississippi Half-Step Uptown Toodeloo; Peggy-O; Tennessee Jed; Black-Throated Wind; China Cat Sunflower > I Know You Rider; Loser; Black Peter; Weather Report Suite (i. Prelude; ii. Part One; iii. Let It Grow) > Stella Blue

1.5: Phil and Ned

2: Me and My Uncle; Dire Wolf; Not Fade Away; Ramble On Rose; Big River; Dark Star > Morning Dew; Sugar Magnolia

E: US Blues

YOU KNOW WHEN you know. You can understand it, somebody can tell you about it, it can be spray-painted in Day-Glo orange on the wall outside your bedroom window, but you don't know it until you know it. Until you *feel* it. The Grateful Dead had never toured longer or harder or performed before more people, so why were they broke? Answer: the Wall of Sound. They'd also never played better—more consistently or more adventurously—so why were people in management and among the crew threatening to quit, and why were band members sniping at each other? Answer: drugs, principally cocaine.

Just when everyone was wishing there was something stronger than a cup of coffee to help get them through the day (and most of the night), along came the coke. People didn't refer to it as "Vitamin C" for nothing. It wasn't long, however, before some Grateful Dead insiders began to see the drug as no longer part of the solution—an occasional pick-me-up to facilitate longer hours and more work, as it had been used in the past—but as part of the problem. This wasn't like sharing a joint with friends or exploring inner space via a psychedelic. Cocaine—at least how it was employed, by this point, by many people in the world of the Dead (who only did moderation in moderation)—was a '70s drug, a go-go-go, me-me-me drug. Talking to biographer Blair Jackson for his *Garcia: An American Life* (the best book written not just about Garcia, but about the Grateful Dead), Garcia's second wife, Caroline (a.k.a. Mountain Girl), recounted how "If anything ruined our lives it was cocaine. Jerry and I had fights about it. Coke makes you think you know it all and it makes you shoot your mouth off and it makes you hate everybody the next day. It was the end of the open heart." It would be disingenuous, however, to say that for a long time, cocaine didn't help keep the train on the track and rolling down the line.

Which is where they were and what they were doing on August 2, 1974, at Roosevelt Stadium in Jersey City, New Jersey, when, according to Dennis McNally's *A Long Strange Trip: The Inside History of the Grateful Dead*, the weather turned nasty, and so did the crowd. Drawing the short stick, Weir was in the process of explaining to the assembled thirty thousand that, for safety reasons, they'd have to postpone the gig because of the rain but would return soon to make it up (which they did four days later), when someone hit him with a bottle. The people had been promised a party and the people were not amused. *Rock and roll! Play all night! I betcha Grand Funk Railroad wouldn't wimp out because of a little fucking rain, that's for fucking sure.* Toto, we're not in Marin County anymore.

A month later they weren't even in America—they were in Europe, for a short trip (seven shows in twelve days) to plug the new album, *Mars Hotel*, and hopefully to augment their small but passionate European fan base. At some point during the London run, the bickering and bad feelings became so pronounced, McNally recounts, that Ram Rod, one of their longest serving and most valued roadies (and this was a band where the hired help had almost as much a say in things as the musicians), challenged the entire group and crew to burn their stashes and get back to what was most important: the music. Which, in a touching show of solidarity, everyone promptly did—only to replenish them soon afterward, none quicker than Garcia apparently. But hey, what choice did they have? There's a gig tonight, and because of all the coke, no one's slept in … what month is this? And let's hope the show's sold out. They needed the money. It wouldn't be the Grateful Dead if they didn't insist upon hauling the Wall of Sound over the ocean and squeezing its six hundred speakers into century-old theatres built at a time when an electrical socket was a big deal. At least they had somewhere good to hide their drugs when they went through customs.

As for the music the band played on their brief European sojourn (three nights in London, one in Germany, two in France), the results should have been predictably spotty, at best, if not downright deficient. And perhaps ears more discerning than mine can bear this out, but in spite of everything else going on and going down, dates such as this one, the second show in London, at the Alexandra Palace (built 1875), are good. Very good. The rock-and-roll songs rock, the country songs *boom-chicka-boom* burn, the ballads all build to moving climaxes, and the longer, jammy stuff gets comprehensively jammed out. If there was a list of what constituted a top-shelf Grateful Dead show, all of the boxes for 9/10/74 would be checked. Is there a faintly detectable brittleness, a certain lack of fervour, to some of the performances? Maybe. Does the jamming on a rare stand-alone "Not Fade Away" sound perfunctory at times? A little. But less-than-flawless Grateful Dead is like less-than-perfect sex: it's still pretty good. And the "Dark Star" > "Morning Dew" that constitute a big chunk of the second set are more than that—a lot more.

This "Dark Star" is more introspective than most, almost tender in places, at least until the first verse is sung (after twenty-three minutes!) and it gets good and crazily (if a tad tediously) cacophonous. But up to that point, it's a tinkling, twinkling "Dark Star," a modal marathon through the group's collective unconscious that hints at a mounting need for calm and quiet and mindful contemplation. It's a prolonged timeout from time, and one of only six versions of "Dark Star" performed all year (and which, post-1974, would never be played again in all of its extended, amorphous glory). Maybe it was an inadvertent requiem.

If it wasn't, the "Morning Dew" that flows so sadly sweetly out of it is. Garcia's voice is so warm and honest and unsentimentally matter-of-fact, it rivals his stirring guitar solos for sheer poignancy, which is saying a lot. When he sings the final "I guess it doesn't matter anyway," you can't help but believe him.

10/16/74 – *Winterland Arena, San Francisco,* CA

1: Bertha; Jack Straw; Deal; Mexicali Blues; It Must
Have Been the Roses; Beat It On Down the Line; Scarlet
Begonias; Me and Bobby McGee; Tennessee Jed;
Cumberland Blues; Row Jimmy; Playing in the Band

2: Phil and Ned > Space > Wharf Rat > Space > Eyes of the
World; Big River; Ship of Fools; Truckin' > Going Down
the Road Feeling Bad > Uncle John's Band; Johnny B.
Goode

E: US Blues

SUCCESSFUL BANDS DIDN'T do this. (The Beatles did, but
they don't count—they're the Beatles.) Over the years, Ray
Davies, David Bowie, and plenty of other rock-and-roll nota-
bles announced to the world their retirement from the touring
business (and for some of the same understandable reasons of
physical burnout, creative inertia, and plain old boredom), but
the Dead actually did it, and just as they were reaching their
peak popularity. The Grateful Dead weren't hippies, they were
neo-beatniks (particularly Garcia, the band's conscience), and
there had to be a better reason to tour than simply because
touring was what you were supposed to do. *Supposed to* is supposed to come from within, not from without.

By the summer of 1974, the Dead's band-owned record
company was hemorrhaging cash, the Wall of Sound was costing almost as much money to operate as the group was taking
in employing it, and cocaine abuse was rampant. By the fall
it was obvious to everyone that the group needed to take a

break, to physically recover from the drugs and the demands of the road. To ditch the Wall of Sound and get out of the record-company business and back to making music full time. To psychologically and creatively recharge (nine years playing with the same people is longer than most marriages last and just as challenging). In October they performed five shows over five nights at their old home base Winterland, and no one, not even the band, knew whether or not these would be their final shows as the Grateful Dead. People referred to them as the "retirement shows," and tickets for the final gig carried the portentous declaration "The Last One."

Even on a so-so night, circa 1971–74, the Dead were still pretty great, and if there was a lot going on non-musically at the time that might have understandably distracted—several movie cameras stalking the stage, for instance (if this *was* it, Garcia reasoned, getting their goodbye on celluloid seemed like a good idea)—it didn't stop the Dead from going out in style. All five nights are mandatory listening (and watching: the resultant movie, the typically modestly titled *The Grateful Dead Movie*, is the best way to visually experience the Dead at the crest of their creativity), and there are more than a few very memorable moments throughout the run (the final "Weather Report Suite"; the last "China–Rider" for three years; the last "Dark Star" until New Year's Eve, 1978; 10/19/74's glorious "He's Gone" > "Caution Jam" [which at times sounds a lot like "Truckin'"] > "Drums" > "Space" > "Truckin'" > "Black Peter" > "Sunshine Daydream"; and, well, you get the picture). What makes the first night, 10/16/74, so special is the approximately two minutes of music that occurs during the transition from the space jam in "Playing in the Band" to the song's restatement of its opening theme. God is in the details. So is the glory of the Grateful Dead.

Not that there isn't an abundance of other highlights, especially the colossal second-set opening "Phil and Ned" > "Space" > "Wharf Rat" > "Space" > "Eyes of the World." Depending upon your affection for shrieky electronic skronk, the nearly twenty-four-minute "Phil and Ned" is either heaven or hell, but the jam that emerges after the rest of the band return from the break and join in is long (over twenty-five minutes), strange, inventive, and certainly not what you'd expect from a group intent upon capturing a sufficient number of satisfactory performances to include in their first film. *Sure, we're making a movie*, it seems to say—an expensive movie (*too* expensive, according to some in the band and management, a cause of further friction later on, when the bills started coming in)— *but, hey, why* not *begin the second set of one of only five chances we've got to get it right with close to an hour of improvisational insanity? We can always get that definitive take of "Sugar Magnolia" tomorrow night. Or the night after that. Or the night after that.* The "Wharf Rat" that eventually surfaces is even spookier than usual for its lengthy, jammy gestation, but just when you think you're returning to Earth, a nearly twenty-minute "Eyes of World" propels you back into the stratosphere. The succeeding "Truckin'" > "Going Down the Road Feeling Bad" > "Uncle John's Band" sequence isn't too shabby either. And as an added bonus, Lesh sings Weir "Happy Birthday" in his best faux– Marilyn Monroe before the "US Blues" encore. A Grateful Dead gig was still a party and not yet a concert.

"Playing in the Band" closes the first set by opening right up, the band clearly unable to wait until the second set to slip into their spacey suits and commence sonic exploring. It's over thirty-three and a half minutes long, and not a second of it is wasted, Garcia going gaga on the wah-wah and Lesh illustrating that he was as imaginative a soloist as anyone else in the group. And when it's time to return from the ether, after almost half an hour of spectacular space, the segue back is as gently bubbling gestating as what preceded it was dynamic and fierce. Watch the movie and see Garcia, glasses resting on the tip of his sweaty nose, conduct the band back into the theme. At one point, just before it arrives, he shushes the others, coaxing them into deeper and deeper trembling calm. Which they do. Brilliantly.

Until everyone is dancing again and singing along about playing in the band, playing in the band.

3/23/75 – *Kezar Stadium, San Francisco,* CA

1: Blues for Allah > Stronger Than Dirt > Drums > Stronger Than Dirt > Blues for Allah

E: Johnny B. Goode

OF COURSE, "RETIREMENT" *is* a relative term. The Godchauxs recorded their own LP (*Keith & Donna*), Lesh collaborated with Ned Lagin on an album of electronic music (*Seastones*)—both released on the Dead-owned Round Records—Weir played around town with a cool bar band called Kingfish, and Garcia... Garcia did *everything*.

Aside from helping to edit the miles of film shot at the farewell concerts, he put together his own solo LP (*Reflections*), guested on about a million other people's sessions (including playing all of the guitar parts on Keith and Donna's record and producing, arranging, and instrumentally dominating Hunter's second solo album, *Tiger Rose*, also on Round Records), and went from non-stop touring with the Dead to non-stop touring with his solo band. (And occasionally playing lead guitar with Keith and Donna's band live to help promote their new LP.) There were even some in the Grateful Dead circle who were apparently a little disconcerted to discover that Garcia had booked his solo group for three consecutive nights at The Golden Bear nightclub, a mere five days after the last Winterland show, since he'd been one of the prime movers behind the hiatus in the first place.

And, oh, yeah: the Dead eventually embarked upon sessions for their next album, *Blues for Allah*, for which Garcia stipulated that they write all of the material in the studio, in an attempt to, as he said, instead of synthesizing different musical styles, create a new style.

Between the last Winterland show on October 20, 1974, and their eventual return to full-time touring on June 3, 1976, they also performed four truncated one-off gigs, three of them benefit concerts (and none of them occurring outside of San Francisco). The first—a Bill Graham–organized benefit in support of cash-strapped local high schools on March 23, 1975—was also the shortest, lasting less than forty minutes. (To keep the hype to a minimum—*The Dead are back! The Dead are back!*—they weren't even billed as the Grateful Dead, but as Jerry Garcia and Friends.) Among the others helping out were Santana, the Doobie Brothers, Brownsville Station, Neil Young, Bob Dylan, Joan Baez, and a few members of the Band, but instead of going with the flow and bashing out a few old favourites for a good cause, like everyone else, the Dead performed an instrumental run-through of one of their works in progress (what would become the title track of *Blues for Allah*) interspersed with "Stronger Than Dirt," another vocal-less tune still under construction (although it had been toyed with in concert for awhile). Donna stayed home, but Hart was back in the fold full time as the band's second percussionist after four-plus years away, and Merl Saunders assisted on Hammond B-3 organ and Ned Lagin on electric piano. Three keyboardists and a couple of unfamiliar, weird instrumentals on a nice, early spring afternoon? Sure, sure, why not?

Just *how* weird the Dead's short set must have sounded to the assembled sixty thousand is best understood in the context of what else they were hearing that day. "Smokin' in the Boys Room" and "Helpless" and "Will the Circle Be Unbroken" and "The Weight" and "Listen to the Music" and…"Blues for Allah"?

It's not so much a song—and certainly isn't an open-ended jam-ming vehicle—as it is a collection of odd, near-atonal, individual pieces stitched together by some *very* unconventional Garcia guitar sounds, a Middle-Eastern-tinged concoction of com-plex chords and uncommon tempos. It still sounds in-progress at times—there are no vocals, and there's a certain degree of tentativeness to the playing early on—but, combined with "Stronger Than Dirt," another twisting, teasing dynamo, this is a solid, straight half-hour of hot and knotty, yet still undeniably freaky, funky music, made only funkier by the addition of Merl Saunders' propulsive B-3 (the Dead should have added him to the group then and there).

After that, though, what do you do for an encore? How about a delightfully unhinged version of "Johnny B. Goode," about as 4/4-far away from what had just come before as you can get. But of course. It's the Dead. Still.

8/13/75 – *Great American Music Hall, San Francisco*, CA

1: Help On the Way>Slipknot!>Franklin's Tower; The Music Never Stopped; It Must Have Been the Roses; Eyes of the World>Stronger Than Dirt; Around and Around

2: Sugaree; Big River; Crazy Fingers>Drums>The Other One>Sage and Spirit>Going Down the Road Feeling Bad; US Blues; Blues for Allah

ALTHOUGH A GOOD argument could be made that creating a new style—Grateful Dead style—was what the band did every time they recorded or played live, what became *Blues for Allah* is unique in their already fairly idiosyncratic discography. In fact, it's the closest the group came to capturing in the studio what a Grateful Dead concert is like, particularly the more open-ended second set. And just before the album's release in the fall of 1975, the Dead played its only full-length (if a little brief, at around two hours) concert during the band's eighteen-month vacation, to publicize its arrival in shops. The venue the band chose, the intimate Great American Music Hall (less than a thousand capacity), was inspired, and the invitation-only audience (friends, family, and music-business people) were treated to a real treat. If this was who they were now, there was obviously still a lot of life left in the Dead.

During the course of the show the band played the entirety of *Blues for Allah*—in sequence—interspersed with a few old favourites, and from the first number (the opening track on the new album), "Help On the Way," the Dead are *on*, swinging confidently from one song to the next without pause (as on the L P). The opening, interconnected triptych of tunes ("Help On the Way" > "Slipknot!" > "Franklin's Tower") are slippery, sinewy, and sleek; funky jazz-rock if you require a label, but really just the way the Grateful Dead felt like playing these days. Also new is the fat, fuzzy tone that Garcia occasionally coaxes from his guitar, which contrasts nicely with the overall quicksilver sound of the new music.

Garcia, as usual, is the primary instrumental focus (and not just on the newer stuff, like the lullaby reggae of "Crazy Fingers"; he sizzles during his "Big River" solo), but Keith is delightfully ubiquitous and playing a lot of Fender Rhodes, which meshes wonderfully well with the jazzier timbres produced by the rest of the band. Lesh is his dependably incomparable self—check out his *plunk-plunk-...plonk* work on a slightly slowed-down "Eyes of the World"—and in the quieter confines of the Great American Music Hall, Weir's distinctive rhythm guitar is even more evident and enjoyable (marvel at the multiplicity of his nuanced accompaniment). Even the drums are mostly unassailable ("Going Down the Road Feeling Bad" takes a couple of minutes to find the right tempo), Kreutzmann and Hart an eight-limbed tandem once again, the former typically handling the beat (and keeping it), the latter supplying tasty percussive touches. (In time, they'd come to "share" the basic beat more, and Hart's tendency to play on top of it would prove an unfortunate development.)

Hunter's lyrics also had been composed primarily in the studio and, like the music, are touched with desert dew, and with the occasional unforgettable line mixed in (what happens when you play with ice is a personal favourite). Garcia sings very, very well—committed and clearly delighted to be debuting all of these fresh creations—although even he and

Weir and Donna can't do much with the lengthy, concluding title cut, which is much more successful in its vocal-less
version on 3/23/75 (unless atonal chanting is your thing). It
must have been a bitch to write, learn, and remember, and it's
easy to see why this was the first and last time it was performed
live in its entirety. But they did play it—and even incorporated
the miked sound of actual chirping crickets, as on the record—
because that's what they felt like doing. Because that's what the
Grateful Dead did.

6/9/76 – *Boston Music Hall, Boston*, MA

1: Cold Rain and Snow; Cassidy; Scarlet Begonias; The Music Never Stopped; Crazy Fingers; Big River; They Love Each Other; Looks Like Rain; Ship of Fools; Promised Land

2: St Stephen>Eyes of the World>Let It Grow; Brown-Eyed Women; Lazy Lightning >Supplication; High Time; Samson and Delilah; It Must Have Been the Roses; Dancing in the Street>Wharf Rat>Around and Around

E: Franklin's Tower

THEY'RE BACK—THE DEAD have arisen—and here's how the afterlife is going to be: no more hockey rinks and no more Wall of Sound. When the Grateful Dead decided to resume touring again in early 1976—they missed it, they needed the money, they were the Grateful Dead, what else were they supposed to do?—they announced to their fans that, for the most part, henceforth they were going to forgo arenas and stadiums for theatres and other smaller venues. True, there'd be fewer seats and lower revenues, but there'd also be better acoustics and an overall more-humane feel to the entire experience (for both the audience and the band). They also disassembled the Wall of Sound after only thirty-six shows, as much of a logistical nightmare and financial failure as it had been an indisputable auditory success. You try, you succeed or you fail, you move on to the next experiment. That's the Grateful Dead way.

And if the band was going to go back on the road—and was going to admit that this wasn't just a vocation anymore, it was also a job—they'd do that the Grateful Dead way, too. The venues they booked for their maiden post-retirement tour were both more intimate than what they'd grown accustomed to and acoustically superior. Playing a run of shows at the same venue made for a better-rested (theoretically, anyway), less-road-raw crew and band. And the rented PA system was much cheaper to operate and easier to set up and break down (although still profiting from the dedicated sound team's ongoing research and development). The band also experimented with selling tickets directly to the fans that were on their mailing list. But the biggest change, the one that mattered most, was the band's new musical direction.

It's immediately obvious how much the group benefitted from the closer physical proximity and being able to easily hear each other on stage, plenty of sizzling, intimate interplay characterizing the entire tour, which got underway on June 3, the band's first full-length concert open to the public in eighteen months. It's a bright, punchy sound that's (not surprisingly) consistently energetic, the musicians clearly elated to be playing together once again, as well as playing in front of a wildly appreciative audience. They also freshened up their set list, not only adding several numbers ("The Wheel," "Lazy Lightning">"Supplication," "Samson and Delilah"), but also resurrecting a few others ("St Stephen," "Cosmic Charlie," "High Times," "Dancing in the Street"). Overall, there are more ballads, the songs are generally played at a slower tempo, and it feels like there's a hole in the second set where the long-form jamming and the space voyages used to be, but hey, it's the Dead, it's still the Grateful Dead.

"Cassidy," from Weir's solo album *Ace* of a few years back, is another fresh number, having been debuted back in 1974 but never played since, he and Donna showing what an engaging vocal tandem they'd eventually become. It was at this point that Donna's vocals find their way onto the majority of the band's songs, in part because Lesh's voice was ruined from supplying the high harmony parts for the previous ten years. The numbers from *Blues for Allah* (only a year old at this point) sparkle brightest, particularly the unusual and much appreciated encore choice "Franklin's Tower." (Quite a change from one more "One More Saturday Night" or yet another by-the-book "Johnny B. Goode.") Both sets are shorter than what fans were used to, but when the second set opens with the first version of "St Stephen" in almost five years, no one's thinking about time. Like many of the tunes, it's a slower, more-measured rendering, but very welcome, all the same, and compensation for all of the great songs that didn't make it into the initial set lists ("Dark Star," "China Cat Sunflower">"I Know You Rider," "Uncle John's Band," et cetera). In contrast, "Eyes of the World" is played at a much quicker tempo than in the past, and although Lesh, in particular, is as frisky as ever, it's not an entirely successful alteration, much of its breezy bounce sacrificed to the incongruously frantic rhythm. "Let It Grow" has been shorn of its tender, two-part overture, and it's one instance where the group's slimmed-down sound isn't an improvement.

Aside from "Eyes of the World," the only real jamming takes place during the "Dancing in the Street">"Wharf Rat">"Around and Around" sequence, but to get there, first you have to endure the vocal portion of the opening number. Once you have, Garcia does his best to make it interesting, but the revived "Dancing in the Street" isn't a failure because it's been discofied—"Shakedown Street" has a similar mirror-ball rhythm yet rarely failed to cook—but because the vocal arrangement they worked out was so unbelievably cheesy and annoyingly repetitive (*Dancing. Dancing. Dancing in the street. Dancing. Dancing. Dancing in the street.*).

"Wharf Rat," however, might have gained something since the last time it was played live, back in '74, is a little crispier around the edges, a little more like the song's narrator, a bit more forlorn and foggy and desperate. (Like a lot of Garcia/Hunter songs, it would mutate and mature with the years.) The price of song is becoming what we sing.

7/16/76 – *Orpheum Theatre, San Francisco,* CA

1: Cold Rain and Snow; Cassidy; Deal; Mama Tried; Row Jimmy; Big River; Brown-Eyed Women; Looks Like Rain; Peggy-O; The Music Never Stopped > Scarlet Begonias

2: Playing in the Band > Cosmic Charlie > Samson and Delilah > Spanish Jam > Drums > The Wheel > Playing in the Band > Around and Around; High Time; Sugar Magnolia

E: US Blues

AS JACK KEROUAC reminds us, walking on water wasn't built in a day. By the time the Grateful Dead returned home for a whopping six shows in seven nights at the twenty-three-hundred seat Orpheum Theatre—part of the post-retirement plan to play two or more gigs at the same scaled-down venue, as opposed to a single, more-financially prudent but aesthetically less-rewarding evening at the local sports stadium or multi-purpose dome—they'd begun to resemble who they were going to be next. At its best—and all six nights at the Orpheum are superlative (with all of the attendant rushed or sluggish tempos and blown lyrics and off-key singing that come with most great Grateful Dead shows)—the sound of the Dead in 1976 is a band slowly reimagining itself as it goes along. Beer and creative growth are always best when they're organic.

In addition to wanting to shake things up a bit—both stylistically and in terms of song selection—the less-freewheeling, more-streamlined sound was probably at least in part because the majority of the group were in their early to mid-thirties by this point and understandably lacking something in the space-travel cardio department, the physical and psychological demands of taking the psychedelic sacrament (literally or figuratively) and seeing where it led them simply becoming a little too much. Fair enough and fare thee well. We all get old and Earthbound. So, tired of playing the same long songs in the same ways, as the Dead moved into their second month back on the road, the second-set highlight tended be three or four, or sometimes even five, meaty numbers linked together over the course of an hour or more of often inspired, exploratory playing.

The first sets were pretty swell, too—tight, tough versions of all the usual suspects, plus a little mellow jamming during stretched out versions of tunes like "Row Jimmy" and "Scarlet Begonias"—but the second set was where Dead Heads who worried that their favourite aural astronauts had been permanently grounded had their fears assuaged. And on nights like July 16, 1976, their minds blown, as well. Even though the shows tended to be shorter, and thirty-minute versions of "The Other One" or "Playing in the Band" or the still-absent "Dark Star" had become extinct, just because aesthetic excess was out and (relative) concision was in, doesn't mean there wasn't still plenty of extended musical excitement.

Gone were the days when "Playing in the Band" would sometimes comprise a quarter of the entire second set, but this rendition is still longer than usual, by the standards of the day (nearly twenty-two total minutes of twisting, probing jamming), and provides the bookends to almost seventy minutes of continuous, interconnected thrills. (It also includes the last "Stronger Than Dirt," part of the instrumental suite from *Blues for Allah* entitled "King Solomon's Marbles.") "Cosmic Charlie" (one of only six post-retirement versions before being shelved again, this time permanently) is a slinky, teasing delight. The best things about "Samson and Delilah" are that it's new and that Garcia gets to play some stinging blues licks, while Keith provides a bed of tinkling support; melodically, it's more than a little thin, and its rhythm, like a lot of Weir's tunes and arrangements, even the superior ones, seems unnecessarily busy. The "Spanish Jam" that emerges from it, though, is a smooth, shadowy journey that results in some stellar Española-influenced improvisation which even the resulting "Drums" can't dilute (think *Bitches Brew*–era Miles Davis). Besides, out of the *boom boom boom* bedlam comes an absolutely stunning "The Wheel," the rainbow after the storm, the cooling beauty of Earth after the Big Bang *bang bang*. In a better world, this would be in every religion's hymn book, the existential mystery of human doing and being all wrapped up in a tidy little package of sighing enchantment.

When the familiar circling chords of "Playing in the Band" emerge from the mist of "The Wheel" the journey there and back is complete—almost. "Around and Around" might seem like an afterthought after so much near-ethereal playing, but it works, gets everyone's feet firmly planted back on the ground, and in the process inspires the band to keep going, "High Time" an unusual late-set choice, but welcome for that very reason, and "Sugar Magnolia" a dependably rapturous send-off. Until the encore "US Blues."

It was 1976, after all: America's Bicentennial. And what was America but a country that invented and constantly reinvented itself? And what could be more American than the good ol' Grateful Dead? Give me five, I'm still alive.

7/17/76 – *Orpheum Theatre, San Francisco,* CA

1: Promised Land; Mississippi Half-Step Uptown Toodeloo; Mama Tried; Deal; New Minglewood Blues; Peggy-O; Big River; Sugaree; Johnny B. Goode

2: Samson and Delilah; Comes a Time>Drums>The Other One>Eyes of the World>Going Down the Road Feeling Bad>One More Saturday Night

E1: US Blues

E2: Not Fade Away

THERE'S A PRICE to be paid for doing what you want to do, just as there is for doing the right thing, and it doesn't take an accountant specializing in the music business to determine that it makes more economic sense to perform once before an audience of 13,200 people than it does to play the same city six separate times, each before audiences of 2,200. And the cost isn't only monetary or logistical. No matter how young or zealous you are, it would take an extraordinary amount of energy and commitment to simply *attend* six Grateful Dead shows in seven nights; when you're talking about *performing* those same shows—and performing them like the Grateful Dead did, without a song list, without a road map, without a net—the price (physical, psychological, and creative) is incalculable. But that's what the Dead did July 12–18, 1976, because one of their credos when they returned to touring was: less is more. It might not have been a prudent move financially or physically, but it certainly paid off artistically.

Maybe because it's the fifth of six gigs in seven nights, but 7/17/76's first set is even more of an extended warm-up than most Dead shows, featuring a set list heavy on uptempo, over-played Weir numbers ("Mama Tried," "New Minglewood Blues," "Big River") and containing not one but *two* Chuck Berry covers (to open and close). Lengthy, lively versions of Garcia's "Mississippi Half-Step Uptown Toodeloo" and "Sug-aree" (especially) ensure that not all is lost, but this one, even more than most Dead shows, is all about the second set. It opens with "Samson and Delilah," a song chiefly memorable because its *If I had my way* chorus is repeated so many damn times, but after that, and until the double encore, it's one long mind melt. Even the fact that Donna is inexplicably absent for the entirety of the second set can't ruin the fun. Who knows? Maybe that's one of the reasons why the non-stop instrumen-tal interplay is so consistently hot. When one of your team-mates goes down, it's up to everybody else to pick up the slack and play a little harder.

"Comes a Time," to me, is one of those *almost* songs—it almost works: because of its mournful, pretty music, its searching words, its near-glacial grandeur—but in the end, it's a little too close to "Ship of Fools" melodically; and lyrically, the "blind man" line is groan-worthy every time. But none of that matters tonight, because at sixteen minutes, this one is all about the delicate but dedicated jamming. (Garcia's the star, naturally, but Keith comes in second with plenty of shim-mering Fender Rhodes, an instrument he didn't play nearly enough.) Over time, some songs reveal themselves to be mod-el improvisational vehicles, and "Comes a Time" (which the Dead had been playing off and on since late 1971) wasn't one of them (too slow, too minor-key melancholy). Except tonight it is. This is one of the virtues of travelling without GPS: you might get lost, but the road you do end up taking just might be more interesting.

After a short (hurray!) drum break, "The Other One" starts out suitably thunderous but soon slips into more deep space for ten or so delightful minutes. (More than most '76 shows, this one has a distinct '73 or '74 flavour to it.) The next number, "Eyes of the World," is similarly structured (or unstructured): a few captivating, if too brisk, minutes of the song itself (which is just as well, because without Donna's high harmonies, it isn't nearly as successful vocally), then several more minutes of wildly exploratory playing (including, just before song's end, some cosmic chicken-scratching from Garcia). After that, and after "The Other One" is revisited and rapturously wrapped up, it's a "Going Down the Road Feeling Bad" > "One More Saturday Night" sandwich to take home with you in case you get the musical munchies later on and feel like tapping your toes. *Mm, mmm, good.*

But it *is* Saturday night, and they *are* playing in their hometown, after all—and don't underestimate the appeal of sleeping in your own bed and making music for familiar, friendly faces. Familiar, friendly faces you don't have to squint to see. A smoking "US Blues" would have been enough—they'd been playing for nearly a week straight, don't forget, and there was still one more night to go—and that might very well have been their intention, to say goodnight after their Bicentennial head-bobber, but "Not Fade Away," the rare second encore that follows, is long (fourteen minutes) and exultant, definitely not a perfunctory run-through to placate the fans. The art you give yourself always makes for the best gift.

7/18/76 – *Orpheum Theatre, San Francisco,* CA

1: Mississippi Half-Step Uptown Toodeloo; Cassidy; Row Jimmy; Mama Tried; Scarlet Begonias; Looks Like Rain; Tennessee Jed; New Minglewood Blues; Loser; The Music Never Stopped

2: Might As Well; Samson and Delilah; Candyman; Lazy Lightning > Supplication > Let It Grow > Drums > Let It Grow > Wharf Rat > Drums > The Other One > St Stephen > Not Fade Away > The Wheel > The Other One > Stella Blue; Sugar Magnolia

E: Johnny B. Goode

IN HOCKEY IT'S called a natural hat trick, lighting the lamp three times in a row. And the third one, 7/18/76, might be the most impressive marker of all, the goalie deked out of their jockstrap and lying flat on their back on the ice and the puck buried in the top right corner of the net. Helping propel the band to the finish line in style was not only the prospect of two whole weeks off the road until the next gig (except for Garcia, of course, who was playing two nights later with his solo band at the Keystone), but also the fact that portions of the show were being recorded for a nationally aired FM-radio broadcast, part of the Dead's continuing strategy to keep attendance at their shows down to a civilized number, so that everyone would have a better time. Everything exists in an ecosystem, even the Dead, and fewer people meant better music meant a happier band meant happier fans meant a happier band. And happy is why we're here, isn't it?

Although, as usual, it's a solid opening set that ranks behind an astonishing second set, Garcia won't let it become merely competent, "Mississippi Half-Step Uptown Toodeloo," "Row Jimmy," and "Scarlet Begonias" all bursting with ingenious lead guitar little twists and turns and compelling chords and unusual changes that make them all, also as usual, absolutely unique and mandatory hearing. And how reassuring to get "The Music Never Stopped" to close out the first set; almost as stirring as hearing "Might As Well" open up the second, Garcia and Hunter's rollicking, *carpe diem* ode to the famous Festival Express tour that took the group and a trainload of other lucky music-making lunatics across Canada in the spring of 1970 (captured for posterity on the excellent *Festival Express* documentary) the perfect tune to get the party going again.

By now the post-retirement template for the evening's second-set festivities had been set: a few tunes ("Candyman" is especially agreeable, even without the bewitching treated-steel-guitar solo Garcia played on the studio version), plus a few more tunes stitched together and jammed around and inside and upside down and across, but tonight it's more than a few—a lot more. How much more? Over an hour of "Lazy Lightning">"Supplication">"Let It Grow">"Drums">"Let It Grow">"Wharf Rat">"Drums">"The Other One">"St Stephen">"Not Fade Away">"The Wheel">"The Other One">"Stella Blue" more, that's how much. It wouldn't be the Dead, though, if it was all about what it seemed. Some of the most interesting parts of this epic sequence are contained in the segues between songs, the spontaneous construction of absorbing musical bridges connecting one tune to the next. Come for the songs, stay for the segues.

"Lazy Lightning">"Supplication" was never about the tune(s), which is slight, but about its tempo-shifting tension and the space it provides for Garcia and Weir to exhibit their six-string, jazzy joy. A brief but tasty transition leads to a less vigorous (and perhaps improved) "Let It Grow," and after a dual drum solo that benefits from the addition of Hart's four busy limbs, it's back to a "Let It Grow" whose finest moment is its outro, a rich collection of sometimes-familiar, sometimes-unfamiliar, but always-intriguing sounds. "Wharf Rat," where it eventually ends up, is a stunner, one of those spooky Grateful Dead moments (usually courtesy of one of Garcia's ballads) where the on-their-feet crowd stops moving and stops cheering and stands and sways and enters the shadowy, sublime world of the Garcia/Hunter songbook.

The transition into "The Other One" is a snaky charmer and the highlight of the entire bisected number. The Dead didn't take requests, but if I had my way, there would have been fewer inessential Weir tunes (how many times can you listen to "El Paso" or "Mama Tried" or "Samson and Delilah" and not wonder why you're listening?) and more open-ended conversations like these, more uncharted trips to who-knows-where. But artists aren't jukeboxes. Thankfully.

The "St Stephen" that emerges out of "The Other One" is one of the slowest, if not *the* slowest, versions the group ever performed—so slow, at times it almost sounds like a different song, which might have been the point—but when those familiar first notes filled the Orpheum, no one was complaining that it wasn't peppy enough. Imagine the Rolling Stones performing "Start Me Up" in waltz time and you understand why people say that there's nothing like a Grateful Dead concert.

And there's more—a lot more: a similarly slowed-down "Not Fade Away" (one tune that probably should always be cranked up and out), a typically rapturous "The Wheel," a soft-landing resumption of "The Other One" (which could use a little more raunch) and… "Stella Blue." It's not as magnificent as the versions from 11/4/77 or 10/20/78, but then what version is? Garcia's guitar is at its sparkling, single-note, soul-piercing best, and vocally, it's as if, two years after debuting it, the words are starting to make sense, it—*life*—really does melt into a dream. A dream that deserves to be danced to. Appropriately, then, to wrap things up, a rip-roaring "Sugar Magnolia."

As Bob Cole used to say on Hockey Night in Canada, *Oh, baby!*

2/26/77 – *Swing Auditorium, San Bernardino,* CA

1: Terrapin Station; New Minglewood Blues; They Love Each Other; Estimated Prophet; Sugaree; Mama Tried; Deal; Playing in the Band>The Wheel>Playing in the Band

2: Samson and Delilah; Tennessee Jed; The Music Never Stopped; Help On the Way>Slipknot!>Franklin's Tower; Promised Land; Eyes of the World>Dancing in the Street>Around and Around

E: US Blues

GARCIA FAMOUSLY TOLD an interviewer that the Grateful Dead's music was like licorice: listeners tended to either hate it or really, really like it. "Terrapin Station" is my *green* licorice. I liked licorice—I even liked black licorice, although, as with most people, I preferred red—but green licorice? Green licorice was akin to roasted-chicken potato chips or vanilla Coke—why? Why mess with a good thing? As stylistically wide-ranging and *out there* as the Dead had ever gotten—the deep-space slow dance of "Dark Star," the brocaded lyrics of "China Cat Sunflower"—they'd never gone prog (although "The Eleven" might have come close). Progressive rock was ostentatious, orchestral-tinged rock music with sub-Tolkienesque lyrics, and what could be less *aw-shucks* Dead than the laughable pomposity of Emerson, Lake & Palmer or *Atom Heart Mother*–era Pink Floyd? Yet here was "Terrapin Station," almost imperial in its slow-building, chorusless musical construction, wedded to words that, even for Hunter at his most profligate, were a little rococo ripe, with its tale-of-yore tone and references to lions' dens and ladies with fans. Green licorice. Yech. Who needs it?

I do—you do—we do. Chemically created jade junk food should only be consumed in small portions, but if it exists, why not give it a try and enjoy whatever pleasures, however less than perfectly nourishing, it provides? As William Blake wrote—I'm quoting from memory, I might be a bit off—*The pride of the peacock is the glory of God and so is green licorice.* As was their way, the Dead debuted a couple of new songs in their inaugural concert of the year, 2/26/77, and "Terrapin Station" was among them. Unusually for them, they'd been off the road for over a month, recording their latest album, the first for their new label, Arista.

The dream of having their own record label(s) had been eventually extinguished by the band's calamitous financial affairs (by now they'd folded Grateful Dead Records and Round Records, righteous failures both, but pecuniary fiascos nonetheless). Additionally, Garcia was spending a lot of money and hundreds of hours in an LA film-editing room, meticulously putting together what would become, a few years later, *The Grateful Dead Movie*, a concert film based on the retirement shows; and the rest of the group, Lesh in particular, becoming increasingly annoyed with how long it was taking and how much more cash it was costing than had been originally estimated. And the band's business manager, Ron Rakow, whom Garcia had brought into the Dead's circle and supported throughout his tenure, even when some band insiders were concerned with his very un-Dead, business-first ethic, burned the group by walking away with approximately two hundred thousand dollars (about a million bucks in 2023 currency).

Because the band was even more broke than usual, they were happy to sign with Arista, home to, among others, Foreigner and Hall & Oates. The label's president, Clive Davis, insisted that the Dead use AOR-producer-*du-jour* Keith Olson to oversee their first LP for the label. That Garcia, in particular, didn't immediately tell Davis to fuck off is all the evidence one needs to see how much the band's priorities had begun to change.

Their *business* priorities, that is; in concert, where the Dead were always most alive, they were still the good ol' Grateful Dead, not only debuting the brand-new "Terrapin Station" (which would provide the new album's title and be predictably butchered by Olson's heavy-handed employment of strings, horns, and a children's choir, rendering the studio version all but unlistenable), but also Weir and Barlow's "Estimated Prophet." Typically, the Dead didn't wait until they'd worked out all of the wrinkles before performing "Terrapin Station" (it's a little rushed, Garcia's vocal phrasing is still uncertain, and Donna and Weir haven't worked out most of their indispensable vocal parts yet); also, in a quintessential Dead move, they *opened* the show with it: an eleven-minute, structurally complex tune they'd never performed in public before, in the lead-off spot usually reserved for short, pounding rockers like "Bertha" or "Promised land." And then immediately proceeded to rock on out with "New Minglewood Blues," a fun slice of raunchy froth off their first album from way back in '67. Classic Dead.

Weir can't wait to bring his newest composition to show and tell, so it's "Estimated Prophet" only two songs later. Part of Weir's peculiar charm as a songwriter—and why he's such a good foil for Garcia and his folk, rock, country, and blues classicism—is that often his compositions' rhythms are slightly *off*, even a straightforward-seeming rocker like "One More Saturday Night" sounding like Chuck Berry with a limp. "Estimated Prophet" might seem like cod-reggae, but it's more accurate to call it Weir(d) reggae, the lurching, almost undanceable (cf. *pro forma* reggae) rhythm giving it its Weir(d) appeal, particularly in conjunction with Barlow's lyrics, told from the point of view of a delusional street prophet ready and willing to embrace the upcoming apocalypse. (And the rude Mu-Tron guitar effect Garcia uses during his solos is perfect.) The first-set fun doesn't stop there, of course—we're only at the fourth (!) number of the night—although a lengthy (for post-1974) "Playing in the Band" > "The Wheel" > "Playing in the Band" to close out the set is, the new songs excepted, undoubtedly its highlight.

In the second set, the still-dynamic *Blues for Allah* triptych "Help On the Way" > "Slipknot!" > "Franklin's Tower" is another standout; an economical but enlivening "Eyes of the World" includes some crisp jamming; and a leisurely, understated "US Blues" encore wraps it up right. First set, second set, encore: regardless, there's a lot to like. A lot to really, really like.

5/8/77 – *Barton Hall, Cornell University, Ithaca,* NY

1: New Minglewood Blues; Loser; El Paso;
They Love Each Other; Jack Straw; Deal; Lazy
Lightning > Supplication; Brown-Eyed Women; Mama
Tried; Row Jimmy; Dancing in the Street

2: Scarlet Begonias > Fire on the Mountain;
Estimated Prophet; St Stephen > Not Fade
Away > St Stephen > Morning Dew

E: One More Saturday Night

I COME TO praise Cornell, not to bury it. But first, just a little
dirt...

Anyone who doesn't know much about the Grateful Dead
still probably knows about Cornell. That it's, like, dude, the
single greatest Grateful Dead concert ever. Except: (1) there's
no such thing as the single greatest Grateful Dead concert; and
(2) even if there were, this wouldn't be it. Let me explain.

There's no single greatest *anything*. Not concerts, not con-
certos, not political cartoons. Anything that's anything—anything that's organically grown and singularly itself and not
pre-packaged and formulaic—is going to have its own personality and tone and texture. Ask a parent who their greatest kid is.
Exactly. But people do tend to enjoy these *greatest ever* conversations, usually because they can't wait to tell you their greatest
ever (*Who's your favourite writer? Oh? Mine's* ——. *What's your
favourite movie? Really? Mine is* ——). Additionally, when our
ego is wobbly or underdeveloped, there's nothing like cement
shoes to keep us from floating away. Having a favourite this or

that grants us significance and permanence by proxy. (That's the hope, anyway.) If your avowed favourite writer is Proust, well, then, you must be one artsy motherfucker, mustn't you? Why, yes, yes, I am, I most certainly am.

When it comes to 5/8/77, there's another reason why so many Dead Heads rank it number one on their list of most memorable Grateful Dead shows. Many Cornell-ophiles became converts when the famous "Betty Boards" became available among tape traders in the mid-1980s, when decent-sounding bootlegs were the exception, not the rule. Bear (Owsley Stanley) was the first person to record the Dead's shows, and his mixes are just fine, if a little lacking in bottom end for my taste, probably because his priority was mixing the band's instruments so they'd sound good onstage. When Bear went to jail for practising his other trade—making the best LSD known to humanity—Kidd Candelario and Rex Jackson, two of the band's longest-serving roadies, picked up the slack, and the tapes they're credited with are very good, as well (especially considering that they're all just simple two-tracks). But Betty Cantor-Jackson's tapes sound so rich and invitingly warm, it's as if you're right there, right on stage. (And in a wonderful bit of Grateful Dead irony, Cantor-Jackson claims that her tapes sound the way they do because, basically, she mixed the band to sound good in her headphones. The Dead's best music sounds the way it does because, foremost, they played it so that it would sound good to them.) Many people tend to confuse the quality of the tape with what's *on* the tape.

Not that 5/8/77 isn't a wonderful show. It is. Uncommonly tight, after spending all of January and much of February in the studio, recording *Terrapin Station*, their first record for Arista, under the supervision of company-appointed producer and super-stickler Keith Olson, there were plenty of excellent new songs to present and polish, as well as an ample desire to hit the road, after a month and a half stuck inside of a sterile, audienceless recording studio. Every show they played in May '77 is a keeper (some people who like to rank such things actually prefer the next night, in Buffalo), but there *is* something special about Barton Hall, particularly with the commencement of the second set.

After an energetic, well-played opening set (nothing special, but nothing not just fine, thank you very much), whatever claims Cornell has to elite-show status begins with a smoking "Scarlet Begonias" > "Fire on the Mountain" to open the second set. Sure, Garcia screws up the words to "Fire"'s second verse, but what's a little vocal miscue when the playing—particularly the transition—is so inspired? (And why, oh, why couldn't the drummers play this consistently every night?) A stand-alone "Estimated Prophet" is vigorous and appropriately overzealous, but "St Stephen" > "Not Fade Away" > "St Stephen" > "Morning Dew" clinches the deal. "St Stephen" is played at such an agreeably mellow pace, at times it sounds like they're going to slide into Steve Miller's "Take the Money and Run." To keep their catalogue fresh, the Dead would periodically tinker with the arrangements of their songs, particularly the tempo. Sometimes this doesn't work (a sped-up "Loser" loses much of its mournful allure); sometimes, as here, with an almost–waltz time "St Stephen," it does, superbly. "Not Fade Away" is also slowed down (slowed *way* down), as well as being long (over fifteen minutes) and lively—Lesh's descending-bassline shenanigans in the intro are a real treat. There aren't many "Not Fade Away"s that contain this much generous jamming.

Which eventually gives way to "Morning Dew." What began way back in '67 as a protest song has aged into an elegy; not an empty indictment of human stupidity, but an achingly poignant musical poem of irredeemable loss and acceptance. Garcia never sang better, and he just plays and plays, as if he's trying to work out a problem that he knows has no solution. Don't tell anyone, but I think it's the greatest version of "Morning Dew" that the Dead ever played (5/26/72 at the Lyceum coming in a close second). Not that I believe in such things.

5/19/77 – *Fox Theatre, Atlanta,* GA

1: Promised Land; Sugaree>El Paso; Peggy-O; Looks
Like Rain; Row Jimmy; Passenger; Loser; Dancing in the
Street

2: Samson and Delilah; Ramble On Rose; Estimated
Prophet; Terrapin Station>Playing in the Band>Uncle
John's Band>Drums>The Wheel>China Doll>Playing in
the Band

IT'S A DIFFERENT sound with plenty of different songs, but
spring '77 resembles Europe '72 in one fundamental fashion:
it's hard to pick out highlights, because they're *all* highlights.
A partial tally of primo shows from the month of May alone:
Boston 5/7/77. Cornell 5/8/77. Buffalo 5/9/77. Saint Paul
5/11/77. Chicago 5/13/77. Tuscaloosa 5/17/77. Florida
5/21/77. Richmond 5/25/77. And Atlanta 5/19/77. Is it a
perfect show? Of course not. That's part of what makes it art.
Every Big Mac is perfect. Every *untauntaunta* produced by a
drum machine is perfect. Every can of Coca-Cola is perfect.
Perfectly the same, perfectly predictable, perfectly pedestrian.
What we want from our art—what we need—isn't perfection;
what we want is evidence of life—actual life. Of something
never not changing and constantly evolving and always capable of surprising and even, occasionally, astonishing. That's
spring '77. That's Atlanta 5/19/77.

A "Promised Land" opener and there you go, there you are:
what could be more like life than big expectations promptly
extinguished by an overplayed rock-and-roll song (if full of
urgency and energy), performed by a group of musicians

whose strength is certainly not rocking and rolling. And then, also just like life—sometimes, anyway, when we're lucky—a "Sugaree" to return to again and again, a sixteen-minute (!) masterpiece that's second out of the chute. It's not just its uncommon length that distinguishes it, either; it's a mini-symphony of searing, sweet-toned twang with three blurry movements that rise and fall and rise again, a multiple-orgasmic, first-set stunner. Then "El Paso" and we're back to the glaringly prosaic; until a double shot of a very pretty "Peggy-O" and a typically stirring "Looks Like Rain" (the final notes that Weir and Donna hit at song's end are astonishingly powerful). You get the picture. The Good Lord Noise giveth (a silky-shrewd "Row Jimmy" containing some very moving Garcia guitar playing); the Good Lord Noise taketh away (with "Passenger," a song Lesh reputedly wrote so that the band's guitar players would have something really raunchy to play—too bad he didn't write something that didn't sound like just about any bar band anywhere cranking it up to eleven).

And maybe that's it, that's today's weather, that's just the way it goes: overcast ordinariness with intermittent brilliance. "Loser" is a victim of the drummers' increasing tendency to rush the beat. "Dancing in the Street" contains some virtuoso jamming, but is still "Dancing in the Street." Ditto "Samson and Delilah" but without the jamming. "Ramble On Rose" and "Estimated Prophet" are more like it, even if the former is slightly sabotaged by some heavy-handed timekeeping, and the latter is a little less wild-eyed fanatical than usual. What are you going to do? You can complain, but who's going to listen? The sky and the clouds and the sun are going to do whatever they're going to do, anyway. All you can do is take an umbrella with you and hope you don't have to use it.

Day is done, but dimming evening is just coming on, and what's this? An impeccable "Terrapin Station" that flashes bright as inspiration then fades with the fading light. Into a high-speed "Playing in the Band" that quickly rights itself by diving directly up into deep space and staying there for eleven gravity-defying minutes. Into "Uncle John's Band," the concluding verse first, then bam! right into the first verse and we're off in earnest, a nearly twelve-minute supercharged sermon in spite of, or maybe because of, the rising tide and all the things we've got to talk about. Into five minutes of "Drums" (overlong, but building, building, building…) into, mirage-like, a dreamy, leisurely (Garcia doesn't stop soloing and start singing until 2:45), sublime "Wheel." *Sublime*. Into the soft stirring of "Playing in the Band" again and—But wait, no, Garcia doesn't feel like it, wants to keep going, isn't ready to go back to the beginning and finish what they started, works his way into the gorgeously disturbing opening to "China Doll" instead, over and over, until everyone's on board, and the first version of this song to be performed in concert in nearly two and a half years is alive again. *Then* back into "Playing in the Band"—for ten and a half more minutes. This is no perfunctory wrap up: Garcia's guitar doesn't want to stop soaring and searching, and no one else wants it to, either. When it's all done, sixty-five straight minutes later, no one who'd been listening would even want an encore.

It's night now. It's dark. And you know what? It's been a good day. A really, really good day.

5/25/77 – The Mosque, Richmond, VA

1: Mississippi Half-Step Uptown Toodeloo; Jack Straw;
They Love Each Other; Mexicali Blues; Peggy-O; Cassidy;
Loser; Lazy Lightning>Supplication; Brown-Eyed
Women; Promised Land

2: Scarlet Begonias>Fire on the Mountain; Estimated
Prophet>He's Gone>Drums>The Other One>Wharf
Rat>The Other One>The Wheel>Around and Around

E: Johnny B. Goode

ALL THE YEARS combine, indeed. Spring '77 is rightly considered a Grateful Dead touring high point, and one of its most
appealing characteristics is its multifarious makeup, the way
that different eras of the Dead seem to fuse together to create
a whole new sound, the sound of spring '77. Even more so than
some of the season's better-regarded shows (hello, Cornell),
5/25/77 combines the improvisational allure of 1969–74 with
the conspicuously less spacey, but rock-solid, post-retirement
sound with the 1-2-3 tightness of '72 with something new, a
whiff of middle-age melancholy (Garcia was thirty-four, Lesh
thirty-seven), a tingling awareness, conscious or not, of time's
thumping ticking. Spring '77 is an excellent vintage. Blended,
sure, but delectable nonetheless.

Opening with a ten-minute "Mississippi Half-Step Uptown
Toodeloo" is the first indication that this isn't just another whistle stop along the way (the Dead would play nineteen shows in
the month of May alone). Not just because it's not "Bertha" or
"Promised Land" or any other archetypal get-the-band-grooving,

get-the-crowd-moving, lead-off number, but because of Garcia's punctilious vocal delivery (always a sure sign he's "on") and the *Across the Rio Grande-eo* outro which goes on and on, Donna and Weir clearly getting off on each sumptuous sing-along verse as much as the song's composer. "Jack Straw" is fiery and feisty and has gained a not-unbecoming edge; "They Love Each Other" has slowed down and grown up and delights; "Cassidy" is still new enough to sparkle; "Loser" doesn't suffer from the sped-up tempo and heavy-handed thumping that it occasionally did these days; "Peggy-O" is gentle shelter in a storm of electricity; and "Lazy Lightning" > "Supplication" rarely sounded better—still not much of an actual song(s), but a welcome, winding vehicle for the entire band, and Garcia in particular, to play some taut, peppy jazz. When he's right— which he clearly is this evening—Garcia thrives on playing as many different kinds of music as possible, and the first set all by itself provides him with the opportunity to jazz it up, folk around, twang and tease, and rock and roll. It's only an appetizer, though. The main meal is a three-course feast.

"Scarlet Begonias" > "Fire on the Mountain" is a big banquet all by itself, the long, slow transition from "Scarlet" to "Fire" full of enough interesting little licks and quirky changes and melodic variations to keep one coming back for seconds and thirds and fourths. The entire thing, all twenty-one and a half minutes of it, is jammed out post-retirement style—over, around, and underneath the song's throbbing rhythm, all of the instrumental interplay taking place *within* the song—and not, as was often the case in the past, outside of it (as when a twenty-one-minute "Playing in the Band" could be broken down into three minutes of song, fifteen minutes of jamming, three minutes of song). Unlike most of '76, however, the jamming isn't tentative or token; this is raw, reaching stuff. Some people prefer their jamming more open-ended and spacey, others like having a song to hang onto when the fretboard fireworks get started, but when the band is truly cooking, as they so frequently were in the spring of '77, they're both equally delicious, the difference between two big scoops of mint chocolate-chip ice cream in a cone or in a bowl. Either way, who's complaining?

Aside from the pointless "Johnny B. Goode" encore (fun if you were there, I'm sure; forgettable if not), the remainder of the entire show—"Estimated Prophet">"He's Gone">"Drums">"The Other One">"Wharf Rat">"The Other One">"The Wheel">"Around and Around"—is an extended orgy of great songs intertwined with consistently inventive, non-stop jamming. Just one highlight: after fifteen rampaging minutes of "The Other One," Weir keeps attempting to lead the band into the calmer waters of "Wharf Rat," but Garcia won't hear of it, he simply won't have it, ignores Weir's harmonic hints and continues to squelch and squeal and search for a sound he hasn't heard yet, and will not hear until he finally plays it.

He eventually gives in, and we do get to hear about ol' August West and his bottle of burgundy wine and his long, sad tale of down-and-out wharf-rat woe. And is it just me, or does Garcia sound just a little bit like August himself these days? If so, it suits the song, at least, Garcia's body and August's soul two increasingly weary entities (Garcia might have been only thirty-four, but like many hard-working, hard-living, high-achieving individuals, he put more time into the years than most people). After that, it's back to another bracing blast of "The Other One," and then a wonderful "The Wheel" followed by a fun "Around and Around" to get everybody dancing before the lights come on and it's time to go home.

Time for the audience to go home—the Dead were booked into the Baltimore Civic Center the following evening. That they played another outstanding show just twenty-four hours later is impressive enough; that they included only *one* song that was performed twenty-four hours before in Richmond ("Estimated Prophet") is remarkable. Maybe it shouldn't be. It was Spring '77, after all.

10/29/77 – *Chick Evans Field House, Northern Illinois University, DeKalb, IL*

1: Might As Well; Jack Straw; Dire Wolf; Looks Like Rain; Loser; El Paso; Ramble On Rose; New Minglewood Blues; It Must Have Been the Roses; Let It Grow

2: Bertha > Good Lovin'; Friend of the Devil; Estimated Prophet > Eyes of the World > Space > St Stephen > Not Fade Away > Black Peter > Sugar Magnolia

E: One More Saturday Night

SPRING '77 GETS most of the huzzahs, but the Dead's fall tour of that year has its own flavour and its own unique appeal as well. Some of the eager ambition of the spring has perhaps diminished by this time, replaced by slightly less-adventurous set lists and scaled-back jamming and less-nuanced playing, but on certain nights, such as this one, there's something special that sets them apart from merely very good shows (of which the entirety of 1977 is full). Check that: a *lot* of special things. A long fall tour found the band in suburban Illinois two days before Halloween, fresh from a gig in Kansas the night previous, and just a stop along the way before embarking for their next show in Indiana the following night. The schedule was punishing, the world was changing (and not necessarily for the better), the years were adding up, and the road was taking its toll, but on the right night the good ol' Grateful Dead could still be the good ol' Grateful Dead. A night like tonight.

Finally tuned up and ready to go, the audience already up on their feet and ready to rock and revel, "'Might As Well'?"

Garcia asks no one in particular, to which someone in the band answers, "Might As Well," and that's it, off they go. A tune taken from Garcia's most recent solo album, *Reflections* (the members of the Dead were fairly polymorphous when it came to where their songs appeared and whose name was on the front of the record), it's a harder-edged, beefier sound overall that the band is putting out now, but this suits "Might As Well" mighty fine, the band energetically bashing away to the delight of all, including, most importantly, themselves, Garcia going nuts on the "Might as well/might as well" outro as he reaches for notes he can't quite reach and is panting for air that refuses to come and even emits the occasional *whoo*. Wow. Seven minutes in, and Garcia—never the most effusive of vocalists—is already out of breath. That's okay, that's what cigarettes are for.

The tone has been set—no one's holding back anything tonight, blood *will* be spilt by encore time—and triumph follows triumph: "Jack Straw" has grown meatier and mean and gotten better because of it, Weir and Donna's synchronized-shrieking harmonies on the chorus powerful, powerful stuff; "Dire Wolf" is a little too tidy in its heavier, more mainstream arrangement, but is still an irresistible four minutes of frontier fun and boasts a very committed Garcia vocal; "Looks Like Rain" is Weir at his crooning best, and his and Donna's call-and-response vocal work on the coda goes on and on and can't go on long enough. It's moments like these that reinforce how much the Dead benefited from including a strong, high voice in their vocal mix. Rain drops and goose bumps every time.

It's fall 1977, though, not fall '71 or '72 or '73 or '74, so 10/29/77 does have its blemishes. "Loser," to me, is simply unlistenable, is stripped of much of its spooky splendour by the clod-hopping drumming and monotonous tempo. Incredibly, at around the 5:45 mark the beat is sliced in half and very briefly approximates an appropriately measured tempo, but this is unfortunately short-lived. The same sort of sped-up, heavy-handed treatment mars "Ramble On Rose" and "It Must Have Been the Roses," which are both robbed of much of their idiosyncratic rhythmic allure. The clippity-clop country-rock treatment renders all three of them sort of boring, actually, something that (overlong drum solos aside) previously would never have been imaginable when discussing a Grateful Dead concert. And especially on the quieter tunes like "Loser," the cold, clanky sound of the electric piano—which, in place of his preferred Steinway grand piano, Keith was condemned by the group's brain trust to play in the second half of '77—is painful to hear, which at least makes the diminishing number of notes he's playing these days slightly less disconcerting.

Sometimes, particularly as the years roll on and the performances become less and less inspired, a loaded set list can be deceiving, what looks tantalizing on paper turning out to be less than exhilarating on tape, but the "Estimated Prophet" > "Eyes of the World" > "Space" > "St Stephen" > "Not Fade Away" > "Black Peter" > "Sugar Magnolia" here is the real deal, a bona fide late-era classic with its own latter-day personality. "Estimated" is good and crunchy creepy, as it should be, with plenty of menacing Mu-Tron courtesy of Garcia, and is only marred by the annoying beeps and blips and burps produced by Keith's electric piano, which isn't aided by his increasingly monochromatic playing habits. Too many "Eyes of the World"s from this time are played too-frenzied fast, but this one is breezy dreamy and smooth as a stick of warm cannabutter (its only fault being that the beat actually *slows down* after Garcia's first scintillating solo, another victim of the rhythm section's inability to stick to one tempo). "Space," a relatively recent phenomenon, is next and, despite including a couple of interesting Garcia moments, carries a whiff of wasteful wankery, as though the band had decided that if the fans needed a sample of their fearless exploratory past, a pre-designed piece of noise nostalgia would have to do. Hunter S. Thompson famously wrote, "When the going gets weird, the weird turn pro." Only trouble is, when the weird turn pro, the weirdness isn't weird anymore. Not authentically weird.

"St Stephen" is another number that just might be improved in its brawnier, louder, latter-day incarnation, having left behind its perhaps over-precious beginnings to become an off-balance piece of funky-unfunky funk, delirious dance music for the world's flat-footed. Then, after the most seamless introduction to "Not Fade Away" I can recall, Lesh decides to play Marco Polo with the drummers for an entertaining few minutes before leading the charge into a short (7:37) but scorching "Not Fade Away" that sounds like a prayer as much as a promise. If that had been it, it would have been enough, but there's still time for a long, moody, extremely moving "Black Peter" (Keith sufficiently stirred to contribute some cocktail-jazz accompaniment) that is perfectly perversely slotted in between the raving "Not Fade Away" that preceded it and the two out-of-control rockers that wrap things up.

It's not perfect, it's the fall of '77, it's the Dead. It's enough.

1/22/78 – McArthur Court, University of Oregon, Eugene, OR

1: New Minglewood Blues; Dire Wolf; Cassidy; Peggy-O; El Paso; Tennessee Jed; Jack Straw; Row Jimmy; The Music Never Stopped

2: Bertha > Good Lovin'; Ship of Fools; Samson and Delilah; Terrapin Station > Drums > The Other One > Space > St Stephen > Not Fade Away > Around and Around

E: US Blues

AUTUMNAL BEAUTY IS still beauty. Sure, the leaves change colours and the limbs of the trees begin to droop with their sickly sweet fruit, but there *are* still leaves, and fruit *is* still hanging from the branches, and only someone under the age of thirty could fail to see that tragedy isn't a tragedy but is only the sweetly sorrowful way of all flesh and of all middle-aged rock-and-roll bands. And when there *is* beauty—a towering, century-old maple swaying in the breeze, that's only one brawny windstorm away from becoming firewood—it might be even more beautiful.

Omens tend to only make sense afterward, when viewed through the backward binoculars of time, but when the second and third shows of 1978 were marred by Garcia losing his voice due to laryngitis, it's pardonable to retrospectively read the tea leaves and reflect that '78 is the Grateful Dead's demarcation line, the point at which the good times aren't quite so abundant and the only-so-so times seem to occur more often. The two shows in San Diego (1/7/78 and 1/8/78) at which Weir sang all but one of the evenings' numbers (Donna chipped in with her heartfelt but no-less-undistinguished "Sunrise" both nights) aren't without their appeal—how could they be if Garcia was still playing lead guitar all night?—but in spite of the members' justified claims to interdependent musical significance, if Garcia isn't happening, the Dead aren't happening. Period. The whole of the Grateful Dead may be bigger than the sum of its singing and playing parts, but if the Jerry Garcia part is missing or messed up, the whole isn't so big anymore. From 1978 on, those big moments are still there, but you've got to look a little bit harder to find them. And chances are, when you do locate them, they'll probably be courtesy of Garcia.

Whether because of the massive amount of cocaine being consumed all around by this point, or because the band was striving to connect with the people in the nosebleed sections of the hockey rinks they were routinely performing in again now (because it turned out that being a music-first aesthete was a lot easier to pull off when no one had kids and mortgages and expensive drug habits), or because of Mickey Hart and his *oompahpah* tendency to bash out the beat, too many songs were performed too *boom boom boom, boom boom boom* flat and fast and rushed. If the Dead never exactly swung with Kreutzmann as the sole drummer, there was at least *some* swing; too often now, it sounded as if the drummers couldn't wait to get to the end of the more rhythmically subtle songs, like "Tennessee Jed," which consequently loses much of its woozy charm, Kreutzmann and Hart frequently sounding like a gigantic, sped-up metronome. Too often, adagio was out, allegro was in. (Interestingly, in Kreutzmann's memoir, *Deal*, he admits that the best he ever played with the band was

during the Dead's spring 1972 tour of Europe, when he eschewed cocaine from his daily diet for the entire duration of
the visit.) Another anomaly of 1978 was that, contrary to the
Grateful Dead's customary way, no new songs were broken out
during this, their first show of the year.

It wasn't all doom and gloom, of course. July and August
would see the debut of five fresh tunes (three of them pretty
good, two of them pretty forgettable), and later in the year Weir
introduced some greasy "rhythm" slide guitar to the band's
sound, which was almost like adding another lead instrument
to the mix. (Although in a later interview he did hint that the
decision to diversify the group's sound was partially because of
Keith's increasingly apathetic playing. It's impossible to know
whether the band's insistence around this time that he switch
from the acoustic piano and Fender Rhodes he preferred to
the less-warm, more-contemporary—i.e., cheap and artifi-
cial—sound of an electric piano had anything to do with his
worsening mood and playing, but it sure doesn't do much for
the listener's state of mind or ears.) But the best argument for
'78 is the best of its shows. January 22, 1978, is one of them.

The first half is fairly typical of a solid first set from this year:
shortish songs (including the recently revived, slimmed-down
"Good Lovin'"), and not many of them (at least compared to
Grateful Dead gigs from previous eras), and very little colour-
ing outside of the lines, the jamming having to wait its turn
until the second set. (It was around this time that the group
formally debuted "Space," a designated period of musical weirdness during each second set, reminiscent of a long-married
couple attempting to keep the sexual spark alive by dutifully screwing every other Saturday night.) But none of this
matters because of "Terrapin Station" > "Drums" > "The Other

One"›"Space"›"St Stephen"›"Not Fade Away"›"Around and Around."

From the top: "Terrapin" is everything it was intended to be (mysterious, mournful, astonishingly uplifting). "Drums," even at nearly eight minutes, is unusually dynamic and doesn't overstay its welcome. "The Other One"—in particular Lesh's jackhammer bass-guitar introduction—is *ferocious*, a lengthy (for a post-retirement version) piledriving stunner. "Space" (much of which is just Garcia alone with his guitar) is distinguished by the "Theme from *Close Encounters of the Third Kind*" he toys with and eventually briefly unleashes, a strange, and strangely affecting, moment. "St Stephen"—which Garcia slams into without bothering with its twinkling introduction—manages to conjure up an entire long-gone epoch with big, fat, crunchy chords and an irresistible rollicking rhythm (and some scintillating guitar work courtesy of Garcia beginning at around the 4:50 mark). "Not Fade Away" is very long (14:09), very involved (it gets downright jammy at times), and on this night, very meaningful. (Lesh's descending bass line is nice and nasty too.) "Around and Around" is when we kid ourselves that we're still kids, that jumping up and down and singing along as loud as we can is all that matters.

And tonight—right here, right now—it just might be.

2/5/78 – UNI-*Dome, University of Northern Iowa, Cedar Falls,* IA

1: Bertha > Good Lovin'; Brown-Eyed Women; El Paso; Tennessee Jed; Sunrise; New Minglewood Blues; Friend of the Devil; Passenger; Deal

2: Scarlet Begonias > Fire on the Mountain; Samson and Delilah; Ship of Fools; Truckin' > Drums > The Other One > Wharf Rat > Around and Around

E: US Blues

SO YOU WANT to be a rock-and-roll star. How do four tour-ending shows over five nights in Illinois, Wisconsin (twice), and Iowa sound? In February? After having already played fourteen gigs in seven states over the course of the previous twenty-six days? Cold, exhausting, and tedious, that's how. But the show must go on, you can't let down the fans, there's no business like show business. Ergo, Iowa in the middle of winter, at something called the "UNI-Dome." The UNI-*Dome.* JesusfuckingChrist. If cocaine didn't exist, road managers would have to invent it.

Thankfully, there's no need, the snow up everyone's noses almost as plentiful as what's covering the Iowa earth outside; and besides, that's what an opening salvo of "Bertha" > "Good Lovin'" (shorn of its jamtastic dimension) is for, a back-to-back blast of basic rock and roll to get the blood flowing and everyone stumbling awake in the same direction. Which does the job, I guess—here we are, here we go, 1-2-3-4—even if it takes the drummers a while to settle on a single tempo (not that they actually stick to it) and it's more manufactured energy than authentic oomph that gets them through to the end. Ditto the majority of the short (by classic Grateful Dead standards) opening set, "Brown-Eyed Women," "El Paso," "Tennessee Jed," "Sunrise," "New Minglewood Blues," and "Passenger," equal parts too-predictable song selection, unsteady rhythms, and perfunctory performances. Only "Deal" and "Friend of the Devil" impress, the former a fiery reminder that the guy playing lead guitar is, after all, a genius, the latter the only first-set tune (the anemic "Sunrise" excepted) that does what Garcia seems to do best these days, song-wise, the unhurried, slow-building ballad. (Maybe not coincidentally, both tunes also regularly appeared in Garcia's small-club solo shows, where he sounded increasingly more inspired than during his rock-star day job.) Anyway, one set down, one more to go. Sometimes, surviving is success enough.

And then: no fooling around, folks, here we go, "Scarlet Be-gonias" right out of the gate, a bright and bouncy prelude to a lengthy "Fire on the Mountain" (the entire thing totals 29:43). Except that it's *too* bouncy, rushes along at such a panicky pace that it loses a great deal of its easy-going, samba-like swing (Garcia and Donna can barely fit all the words in before it's off to the next verse). Except that by the time "Scarlet" is over, and everyone falls into a good deep groove, and Garcia clicks on the Mu-Tron and slaps down the first *whap whap whap* notes of "Fire on the Mountain," it's goosebump time in Iowa, it's going to take a whole pail of water to cool this motherfucker down. "Fire" simply burns and burns, Garcia taking incendiary solo after solo. (And the lengthier-than-usual segue contains some of the best playing.) By the time it's over, half an hour later, you've forgotten how inauspiciously and even disappointingly it all began. Which sounds like a lot of '78 Dead. Which sounds a lot like life.

The pump having been primed, the engine is revving on all well-lubed cylinders now, if in a markedly 1978 fashion. "Samson and Delilah" is a thunderous, near–heavy metal monster, Garcia the searing, soloing star although it's ostensibly Weir's tune. Everything got louder and harder and faster in '78, which occasionally negated the understated power of some songs, but here it works (it's "Samson and Delilah," don't forget, not "Loser" or "The Wheel"), the sparks flying from Garcia's guitar doing what Weir's vocals never could—*testifying*. "Ship of Fools"—with Garcia and Weir and Donna harmonizing to great effect—sails in at just the right moment and at the right speed, time to slow things down now and let the vocals do the driving.

Until "Truckin'">"Drums">"The Other One," and it's out of the shelter and back into the deluge of electricity. Typical of '78, none are long or jammed out, but what each loses in intricacy and invention, it makes up for in exhilarating aggression. The appeal and the power of '78 is the force of ferocity, the Dead raging against the dying of the light that was the dreams (musical and otherwise) of the 1960s and early '70s. The Dead might be older and fatter and not quite as inspired (sound familiar?), but they weren't going gently into that not-so-good night that was lamestream America either, were going to rage and rage against the UNI-Domes of the nightmare world that was soon to be 1980. (*1980?* What the *fuck*?) "Truckin'" is a gleeful train wreck (in spite of Weir's managing to get all the words right) and all the more delightful because of it (the accompanying referee whistle on the opening notes is a hoot), and the shrimp-sized (8:06) "The Other One" is *pulverizing,* a principled act of aesthetic annihilation. Garcia plays like an angry god.

   "Wharf Rat" is necessary—the calm after the storm, damage undeniably done and time to take spiritual stock—and a vigorous "Around and Around" is not only a nice way to say goodnight, but infused with a great big chunk of good-time jamming and some searing Garcia soloing. "US Blues"—tough and metallic and playfully sardonic—is the encore. The United States blues, oh my oh my. It makes sense.

9/16/78 – Gizah Sound and Light Theater, Cairo, Egypt

1: Bertha > Good Lovin'; Candyman; Looks Like Rain; Row Jimmy; El Paso; Ramble On Rose; New Minglewood Blues; Deal

2: Ollin Arageed > Fire on the Mountain > Iko Iko; I Need a Miracle > All Over Now; Sunrise; Shakedown Street > Drums > Truckin' > Stella Blue > Around and Around

E: One More Saturday Night

WHAT A WONDERFUL idea. What better way to kick off their shoes and lose their rock-star blues and get back to being psychedelic revolutionaries than to play some Grateful Dead music at the foot of the Egyptian pyramids, swapping the All Purpose Dome in beautiful suburban Somewhere, USA, for the shadow of the Great Sphinx. This was Egypt, 1978, when it was still possible to get on a plane and disembark in another universe. The McWorld hadn't reached Cairo yet, but the Dead did, for three nights of shows, the best of which is 9/16/78.

How badly did the Dead desire—how desperately did the Dead *need*—this escapade? For conservatory reasons, they agreed to limit the attendance at each gig to a paltry thousand or so people, some of them adventurous and deep-pocketed Dead Heads, but many of them locals who'd never even heard of rock and roll before. They paid for the entire trip and the production of the shows themselves, to the tune of about $500,000 (about four times that in contemporary coinage).

They also agreed to donate any proceeds to Egypt's Department of Antiquities and to a charity to be selected by President Sadat's wife. The plan was to recoup their costs with a triple-album culled from the three nights, but until then, coming up with several hundred thousand dollars per show out of their own pockets for the privilege of serenading the Sphinx was indication enough that, in spite of the big record company and the big arenas and the bloated rock-and-roll lifestyle that necessarily accompanies them, deep down, they were still the same old Grateful Dead. The spirit was certainly ready and willing. The flesh, on the other hand...

Not to belabour the biographical, but it's common knowledge that Garcia was using heroin fairly regularly by this point, if still usually playing very well. Keith, meanwhile, had also developed an appetite of his own for white and brown powders, which didn't jibe as well with his onstage performance. It's possible to listen to long stretches of Dead shows from this period where Keith is barely detectable. Sometimes it's actually startling when the electric keyboard he was forced to play, in place of his preferred acoustic piano, pops up in the mix, producing a disconcerting feeling of "Oh, yeah, I forgot, there's a keyboard player in the band." The thrilling counterpoint and frilly fills are mostly a thing of the past now, Keith too often content to bang out rote notes on his toy piano, often with one hand, the other one occupied with a cigarette.

Although he was apparently heroin-free for the moment (even the Dead weren't blasé enough to attempt to smuggle smack into the Middle East, particularly as it took a tremendous amount of time and effort and goodwill to gain enough of the Egyptian government's trust to make their pyramid scheme come true), Garcia, according to Blair Jackson's indispensable

Garcia: An American Life, stayed stoned on painkillers during much of the band's Egyptian stay. Painkillers are good at killing pain—that's what they're intended for. They're *not* so good at opening up your mind and putting you in touch with the world around you. At least there was plenty of good local hash to go around.

The Dead filmed much of their three-night stand, and some of it makes for uneasy viewing. Kreutzmann is playing with only one arm (the other one is entombed in a large cast, the result of falling off a horse just before the band departed for Egypt); half the time, Keith appears as if he has nodded off; and Lesh, with his swollen beer belly, looks more like Garcia than Garcia. Only the always-able-bodied Weir and a double-duty-pulling Hart look up for the challenge. Openers "Bertha" > "Good Lovin'" are a shambles, mainly because Garcia appears as if he's stumbling around in a thick pharmaceutical fog, his playing sloppy, his singing shaky. The best thing that can be said about the remainder of the short set is that it gets better as it goes along, Garcia gradually waking up enough by the midway point to put in a competent, if desultory, performance. The band catches fire on "Deal," however, the last song of the set (a good sweat just what their aging bodies and brains needed, perhaps), Garcia making up for lost opportunities with some scalding solos.

On all three nights, the Nubian musician Hamza El Din and a cast of Egyptian vocalists and percussionists took the stage at the outset of set two to perform "Ollin Arageed," a mesmerizing mix of intriguing Egyptian rhythms and delightfully uncommon (to Western ears) vocalizing. Gradually, the members of the Dead congregate back onstage and join in, the primeval music and the crackling electricity making for a swampy segue to a languid but luscious "Fire on the Mountain," the deep antediluvian groove laid down by Hamza El Din et al. the cosmic click track that the Dead faithfully follow for fifteen scintillating minutes. This, finally, is the Dead.

The "Iko Iko" that follows is hot-and-spicy fun (the band, even Garcia—fully awake by now—pantomiming along at points), the "Shakedown Street">"Drums">"Truckin'" >"Stella Blue">"Around and Around" is generally solid and even includes some satisfactory jamming, and a rocking "One More Saturday Night" brings it all back home, just one more slippin'-and-a-slidin' Saturday night wherever you are.

After they returned to the US and listened to the tapes, Garcia and the others reluctantly decided that none of the performances sounded good enough to warrant commitment to vinyl, so the band was in the hole for a lot of money it didn't have to begin with. So much for wonderful ideas. There was only one thing to do: finish up their latest album, the remarkably flimsy *Shakedown Street*, and get it into the shops in time for Christmas. Then get back on the road.

10/21/78 – *Winterland Arena, San Francisco,* CA

1: Ollin Arageed>Promised Land; Sugaree; Passenger;
Ramble On Rose; Looks Like Rain; Stagger Lee; I Need
a Miracle

2: Bertha>Good Lovin'; It Must Have Been the Roses;
Estimated Prophet>Drums>Got My Mojo Working>The
Other One>Stella Blue>Sugar Magnolia

E: US Blues

SOMETIMES A REST is as good as a change. Sometimes it's
even better. Especially when you're old and dope sick and
happy to be home. A month after returning from Egypt, the
Dead played five consecutive nights at Winterland, in their
hometown of San Francisco, a sort of dual celebration of their
Mediterranean adventure and the completion of their upcoming LP, *Shakedown Street.* The bond between the group and its
fans was strong enough that the band felt compelled to share
some pictorial souvenirs with those who'd heard tantalizing
tales of their adventure abroad, so slides were shown on a large
screen at the rear of the Winterland stage, depicting the sights
and (soundless) sounds of their trip, an Egyptian picture book
of the Dead.

There's definitely some extra giddy-up to their playing on
all five nights, particularly on the songs from the new album.
To say that the title track and Weir's "I Need a Miracle" and
Garcia's "Stagger Lee" surpass the sickly slick versions they'd
committed to vinyl is to obscenely understate the case; the
glossy goop on the LP is to the versions they were playing live

as ditch weed is to Acapulco Gold. The studio rendering of the best song on *Shakedown Street*, "Fire on the Mountain," is 3:47; the version they played on October 22, 1978, the last night of the five concerts, is nearly thirteen minutes. Lesh quipped more than once that the group's albums were often just advertisements for their concerts. Enough said.

The last two shows of the run were opened by Hamza El Din, who had also performed with the band in Egypt, and when the group joins him on stage for awhile before segueing into "Promised Land," it's a classic Grateful Dead moment: the ancient echoes of Egyptian folk music meet Chuck Berry's all-American anthem. The remainder of the first set is full of oomph and energy, but like much of their playing at this time, there's less shimmering beauty and more shake, rattle, and roll, the increased aggression in their sound undeniably engaging at times, but occasionally coarsening and slapdash. Among the older songs, "Looks Like Rain" is the clear standout, Weir and Donna's song-ending call-and-response vocals as beautiful as they are heart-rending. *Here comes the rain…*

And then comes the second set. Uptempo tunes such as the "Bertha" > "Good Lovin'" combo are ideally suited to the band's evolving crash-bam-slam style (although the drummers, as usual at this time, tend to play too much or too fast), but the core of the show (not surprisingly) is the marathon "Estimated Prophet" > "Drums" > "Got My Mojo Working" > "The Other One" > "Stella Blue" > "Sugar Magnolia" medley. It's not quantity, though, but quality that makes this long sequence of songs (over an hour) necessary listening; stamina is impressive, but endurance by itself only endures, is only ever necessary, never sufficient. "Estimated" is a lurching beast, "Drums" is tolerable mainly because of guest Lee Oskar's acrobatic harmonica work (hey, it's homecoming week, why not have a few friends drop by?), and "Mojo," if occasionally a sloppy muddle, is an admittedly surprising selection (one of only two versions the band ever attempted) and the night's only real improvisational vehicle (Weir's screechy rhythm slide is a hoot and a half).

Out of this, "The Other One," which *explodes*—rages and rages, Garcia, by song's end, punishing his guitar with uncharacteristic power chords again and again. By the standards of "The Other One"'s 1969–74 heyday, when twenty-five-minute renditions weren't at all unusual, this one is startlingly brief (just over seven minutes), but this only distills its brute power, accentuates the impotent fury embedded in Garcia's brutal attack. What did he know—about himself, about the Grateful Dead, about the world—that the delighted audience that night didn't? Who knows? Probably not even him. But his guitar did.

After the storm, the calm: "Stella Blue." It's everything that the previous song wasn't: tender, sorrowful, otherworldly, and when Garcia's final solo reaches liftoff at around the six-minute mark, it sounds like his soul is crying, it sounds like it's *wailing*. And it's crying for all of us, for everybody listening, even if none of us, including him, have a clue why it's all so terribly sad and yet still so incredibly beautiful. That's okay. His guitar does. And that's enough.

12/31/78 – *Winterland Arena, San Francisco,* CA

1: Sugar Magnolia; Scarlet Begonias>Fire on the Mountain; Me and My Uncle>Big River; Friend of the Devil; All Over Now; Stagger Lee; From the Heart of Me>Sunshine Daydream

2: Samson and Delilah; Ramble On Rose; I Need a Miracle>Terrapin Station>Playing in the Band>Drums>Not Fade Away>Around and Around

3: Dark Star>The Other One>Dark Star>Wharf Rat>St Stephen>Good Lovin'

E1: Casey Jones>Johnny B. Goode

E2: We Bid You Goodnight

THE END OF the year, the end of an era, the end of the line...
One more New Year's Eve found the Grateful Dead at home, as was customary, but this time the celebration was a little different. For one thing, they were also in mourning—for the imminent closing of Winterland Arena, the former ice-skating rink that promoter Bill Graham transformed into a premier concert venue in 1971, and at which the Dead had played countless crucial shows (the "retirement" concerts, for example, as well as their recent "From Egypt with Love" gigs, plus several New Year's Eves). Graham claimed that the venue, built in 1928, was literally falling apart (more than one concert attendee had been hit by falling plaster), and that because the building's owners wouldn't allow him to deduct the cost of repairs from his rent,

he had no option but to close its doors. Graham knew that there was only one band to shut it down in style.

After opening sets by the Blues Brothers and the New Riders of the Purple Sage (and an evening-opening screening of *Animal House*), the Dead came on at midnight and played until it was light outside. They welcomed the New Year with "Sugar Magnolia" and wrapped things up nearly seven hours later with "We Bid You Goodnight." Just because it was a special night, though (it was also broadcast live on the local public television station and later released on DVD), doesn't mean that the Dead didn't need a couple of hours to come to life, including most of the first set. They're undeniably keyed up by the occasion—how could they not be, after Graham appears just before midnight, suspended high above the crowd and riding an enormous joint, while the band is bathed in an avalanche of balloons when the clock strikes twelve?—but there's a sluggish undercurrent to things initially, a lumbering quality to even the best stuff, that is redolent of '78 as a whole. Overplayed songs (and pairings), like "Me and My Uncle" > "Big River," seem to be running on nothing but elbow grease and coke (which might help explain why the former features two very different tempos), and while the Weir-sung "All Over Now" and Donna's "From the Heart of Me" are laudable attempts to liven up an increasingly stale set list, R&B isn't one of Weir's strengths, and the best that can be said about the recent *Shakedown Street* number "From the Heart of Me" is that it's not "If I Had the World to Give."

There are exceptions—once "Fire on the Mountain" finally ignites, it *burns*, the groove thumping deep and delicious, and the forlorn "Friend of the Devil" might even benefit from the transparently fragmented vibe—but even here some dry rot is detectable, Garcia, for instance, seemingly at a loss as to what to play during solo time (as if he's about to scratch his head and ask himself, *I wonder what would sound interesting here?*). Keith is as little there as he can be and still technically be there—if you're listening, and not watching the DVD, it's easy sometimes to forget there's a keyboard player in the band—while a taciturn Donna, meanwhile, looks as if she would rather be anywhere else, trotting off stage the instant her vocal parts are over. (She also looks like she's been crying for about a week straight, which, coincidentally or not, jibes with the biographical scuttlebutt that she and her husband were going through an especially difficult time). But the Dead always take a while to get going; that's what first sets are for. And, c'mon, it's New Year's Eve.

Things heat up with the third song of the second set. "I Need a Miracle," in spite of being kind of dumb and derivative (I can't help but hear an amped-up version of the Everly Brothers' "When Will I Be Loved" whenever the band cranked it out), is always a good greasy time, and this time it softens and sighs into "Terrapin Station," the first goosebump moment of the night. Like all good music, "Terrapin" is whatever the listener hears it to be, and tonight it sounds beaten but unbowed, depleted but determined. The "song" part of "Playing in the Band" is, as usual for '77 and '78, played too fast, but the resulting spacey jam, while only thirteen minutes long, could almost be mistaken for an abbreviated 1972–74 "Playing." (It's obviously a coincidence, but a light fixture crashes to the stage a few minutes in.)

Keeping with the good-old-days feel, the "Drums" that follows is a full-blown percussive orgy, several people wandering on stage and adding to the bedlam by beating the hell out of whatever flat surfaces are handy, while guest harmonica players Matt Kelly and Lee Oskar blow soulful, simpatico harp.

It's nineteen minutes long and I never skip it, so there you go. Keeping with the auld-lang-syne ambiance, ex–Quicksilver Messenger Service guitar-slinger John Cipollina, all dressed up in his best Haight-Ashbury-circa-1968 threads, joins in on a not-to-be-believed "Not Fade Away" that goes on (and on) for eighteen and a half minutes, a chugging symbiotic love song that's a testament to Grateful Dead/Dead Head love. By the time the band tears into "Around and Around" Keith has put down his cigarette and is banging away at the keys with both hands, and Donna is actually smiling while she and Weir playfully pantomime along to Chuck Berry's paean to all-night partying. Tonight it would even prove prophetic.

When the Dead open the third set (at around four a.m.) with "Dark Star"—which they hadn't performed in over four years (since 10/18/74, the third-to-last retirement show)— there's an almost-audible gasp from the assembled Heads, even if it turns out to be a bite-sized "Dark Star" (12:24)>"The Other One" (6:01)>"Dark Star" (1:10) sequence. It sounds like "Dark Star," but it doesn't *feel* like "Dark Star"—feels, unfortunately, like what it is: a brief nostalgic nod to the fans, a rote revival of an adored classic. But the "Wharf Rat" is seedy shining, "St Stephen" smokes like it did back in the day when smokin' music was all that mattered, and "Good Lovin'" even includes a veiled shout-out to long-gone comrade Pigpen, dead for nearly five years now. In the morning, Bill Graham provided breakfast for five thousand people and everyone went home with the sun in the sky.

In 1985 the abandoned Winterland was converted into luxury apartments. According to their website, all units come with incredible views and large closets and granite countertops. There is a waiting list.

9/25/80 – *The Warfield Theatre, San Francisco,* CA

1: Bird Song; Been All Around This World; Dark Hollow;
Rosalie McFall; Monkey and the Engineer; It Must
Have Been the Roses; Jack-A-Roe; Oh Babe It Ain't No
Lie>Ripple

2: Alabama Getaway>Greatest Story Ever Told; Friend of
the Devil; Mama Tried>Mexicali Blues; Loser; Little Red
Rooster; Althea; Jack Straw; Deal

3: China Cat Sunflower>I Know You Rider;
Samson and Delilah; Ship of Fools; Playing in the
Band>Drums>Wharf Rat>Around and Around>Good
Lovin'

E: US Blues

JUMPED, PUSHED, OR perhaps a bit of both—however it
happened, two and a half months after the Dead said farewell
to Winterland, they said goodbye to the Godchauxs as well.
Keith hadn't been a fully functioning, contributing member
of the group for at least a year—a sad end for such an integral
part of the Grateful Dead's greatest era of music—and Donna
has stated for the record that she and her husband were falling
apart both as a couple and as people (too many drugs, too
much travel, too much pressure to be good parents to their
young son at home, as well as good rock-and-roll pirates out on
the road). She's described her and Keith's departure as mostly
a relief, a necessary step on the road to physical, psychological,
and musical regeneration, and would always speak of herself as

a lifelong Dead Head and of her time with the band as a highlight of her life. (Keith wouldn't be so lucky: after getting clean
and working on new music with Donna and others, he died in
a car crash a little over a year later, just thirty-two years old.)
When Pigpen had died, there'd been some question (however
hyperbolically grief-inspired) of whether or not there'd even
be a Grateful Dead moving forward. Not this time.

Brent Mydland was the keyboard player in Weir's solo band
during this period, an energetic, colourful player with a husky,
harmony-hugging voice, and the Dead quickly added him to
the group as a full-time member. From his first gig with the
band on April 22, 1979, just a couple of months after the Godchauxs' final show, it was clear they'd made a solid choice. After
enduring Keith's increasingly somnambulistic tendencies for
so long, Mydland's enthusiastic keyboard work (mostly organ,
with some Fender Rhodes and a touch of synthesizer) must
have been a bracing change; Garcia, in particular, was clearly inspired by the younger man's infectious energy (he threw
himself—literally—into his playing) and vigorous vocals. (I
don't agree, but many Dead Heads would claim that Mydland's
addition gave the band their finest vocal blend ever.) The
sound of the newly constituted band is understandably a tad
stiff overall—Keith had been behind the keyboard for nearly
eight years, after all, and all of Donna's crucial vocal parts needed to be reworked—but the initial results were promising. And
if one can't help but miss the soothing sound of Keith's flowing filigrees and captivating counterpoint, they'd already been
missing for a while now. It was the dawn of a new decade. And
since when have the Grateful Dead ever been afraid of change?

Therefore, 9/25/80, the first of fifteen—count 'em, fifteen—
shows in almost as many days at the cozy (2,300 seats), classy

(opened in 1922) Warfield Theatre. This is more like it. Fuck Iowa February frostbite or Louisiana August sunstroke: stay home, stay focused, stay true to the music. And while we're at it, let's freshen up the set list as well, which *has* become a trifle stale. Ostensibly a celebration of fifteen years together, for the first time in a decade the Dead were breaking out the acoustic guitars and were going to play an entire set of stripped-down originals and Deadified covers. Folk and country and bluegrass had always been at the heart of who the Dead were, so why not dust off a few old favorites and some time-tested cover tunes and get back to their roots on the way to stretching their musical limbs again? After the fifteen shows at the Warfield (wrapping up with 10/14/80), the Dead would repeat the adventure when they settled in for eight nights at New York's Radio City Music Hall. Sure, it was a bit scary—anything new is bound to be, plus there were two full electric sets to be performed after the wooden music wrapped up, and when you're approaching the forty-year mark, nothing is as easy as it used to be—but being nervous is better than being bored. Is a lot more interesting, anyway.

And it *is* a nice change. Charming, chiming, clean and crisp and fresh. Opener "Bird Song" hadn't been heard in seven years and is the indisputable highlight of the opening acoustic set, Mydland's piano expertly answering every ringing Garcia guitar lick, and the entire band unplugged and turned down and tuned in to the quieter, calmer side of the Grateful Dead experience. And what a lovely batch of surprises they took the time to dig up and serve over: "Been All Around This World," "Monkey and the Engineer," and "Rosalie McFall" hadn't been performed in ten years, "Dark Hollow" and "Ripple" in nine, "Oh Babe It Ain't No Lie," never. (In subsequent shows, still more rare treats would be delivered, including "On the Road Again," last heard all the way back in '66, and the gorgeous "To Lay Me Down," which had been inexplicably absent since '74.) Some of the shows were filmed, and the band looks like the music sounds: a bit rusty and a little out of breath at times, but agreeably mellow and certainly happy to be there.

The two subsequent electric sets aren't nearly as successful. With the languorous Keith out and the dynamic Mydland in, the band is definitely livelier, even frolicsome at times, and there's an unmistakable sturdiness to their sound now, as if they've undergone a long-overdue tune-up and acquired a new set of all-weather tires. But Mydland's keyboards occasionally overwhelm the mix, filling in the open spaces that are so much a part of what makes the Grateful Dead's symbiotic sound so rock-and-roll anathema. (Clearly, he's also a dependable harmony singer, but Donna's commanding contribution is missed and can't be matched.) The song selection doesn't help either: aside from Weir's ill-advised blues cover ("Little Red Rooster") and a couple of decent Garcia/Hunter tunes from the band's flaccid new studio album *Go to Heaven* ("Alabama Getaway" and "Althea"), it's the same old, same old, and there's not a whole lot of it, either—not compared to the marathon three- to four-hour shows that were customary for so long.

But the new guy was still new, and the acoustic set was an encouraging innovation, and who knows what next week's or next month's gig will bring? It took the Grateful Dead fifteen years just to get here. What was a little more time?

5/6/81 – *Nassau Veterans Memorial Coliseum, Uniondale,* NY

1: Alabama Getaway>Greatest Story Ever Told; They Love Each Other; Cassidy; Jack-A-Roe>Little Red Rooster; Dire Wolf>Looks Like Rain; Big Railroad Blues; Let It Grow>Deal

2: New Minglewood Blues; High Times>Lost Sailor>Saint of Circumstance; He's Gone>Caution Jam>Spanish Jam>Drums>The Other One>Going Down the Road Feeling Bad>Wharf Rat>Good Lovin'

E: Don't Ease Me In

WHO KNOWS WHY? Or how? How the mood, the playing, the gig itself, goes from just okay to something special. Baseball players talk to their bats when they're in a slump, and gamblers enduring a losing streak take superstition to a whole other level of silliness, but what's a musician to do when the songs start to sound the same and what was once a sacred calling has somehow turned into a career?

The Grateful Dead, who were once synonymous with the counterculture, had somehow become the mainstream. Sure, they were still the Dead—theirs was a different world from that of, say, Aerosmith or the Doobie Brothers—but big arenas, big money, and the big headaches that come along with being a big deal in American popular culture were all a part of the machine that used to be just "the good ol' Grateful Dead." At the peak of their popularity, the Dead not only had growing families to provide for and sixty employees on their payroll, but also took very good care of them all, from the longest-serving roadie to the newest member of the office staff. Somehow, fun lost out to the fiduciary, and Garcia, in particular, found himself becoming what he'd always despised: not only a celebrity, which was bad enough, but also a terribly overworked, self-medicating American businessman who couldn't afford to slow down because too many people depended on him.

A couple of years into the Mydland era, the Grateful Dead had become a fairly consistent, fairly predictable touring machine, dependably delivering the old favourites while managing to squeeze in two or three more-recent so-so songs per show. Occasionally, though, something extraordinary would happen: a sublime guitar passage from Garcia, most typically, or sometimes even a brief, ensemble-achieved moment of musical bliss. May 6, 1981, contains one of those moments. A long, thrilling moment.

By the dawn of the 1980s, rock and roll had grown up and become what it was always destined to be, once it locked limbs with big business: entertainment. Lucrative (for the performers, for the record companies, for the concert industry) entertainment. The Dead certainly attracted a different audience than, say, Elton John or the Rolling Stones, but the only tangible difference between those acts and the Grateful Dead was that Sir Elton and Sir Mick et al. reliably cranked out the hits, while the Dead dutifully delivered nostalgia, a little incense-and-peppermints auld lang syne for the lean, mean '80s. (Not that you can blame people, especially younger people, for flocking to Grateful Dead shows in greater and greater numbers as the 1980s rolled on and greed was officially declared good and the music on the radio—and on TV! I want my MTV!—became pretty and plastic. Wearing tie-dye and gobbling hallucinogens in the age of Reagan could be considered retrogressively pathetic; it could also be viewed as a badge of dishonour to be worn with neo-hippie pride.) And reeling off some of the highlights of the previous fifteen years was what the Grateful Dead were doing on a spring night in suburban New York, when just another show on just another tour turned into a concert to be treasured.

Well, a second set to be treasured. Up until that point, it's a typical early '80s show (taking place at a typical multi-purpose hockey rink) with a predictable set list that's mirrored by much equally stale playing. There are a few exceptions, naturally—Garcia is intermittently brilliant during "Cassidy," "Jack-A-Roe," and "Let It Grow," and Mydland is everywhere on keyboards—but most of the songs seem rushed and the band never gets into a good loosey-goosey Grateful Dead groove and the overall sound is texturally ambivalent. The Grateful Dead is foremost the sound of Garcia's guitar—single-note, crystalline purity—and Mydland's organ is often distractingly buoyant and bouncy, his occasional use of synthesizers aurally incongruous and off-putting. It's like placing a delicate Rodin watercolour inside a plastic Ikea frame. Weir's voice is still strong and urgent (although you wish it wasn't on "Little Red Rooster"), but Garcia's vocals are already a little worryingly wheezy. (Boy, oh, boy, do they miss Donna, particularly Weir, who, even with Mydland's harmony help, simply can't carry the load on such vocally all-out numbers as "Looks Like Rain" and "Let It Grow.") And where's Lesh? Most of the time he sounds less like the lead-bass-playing buccaneer of before and more like a plain old bottom-hugging bassist. Additionally, when the music is otherwise outstanding, the occasional vocal flubs and missed instrumental cues and rushed rhythms don't matter much; when the music is predominantly pedestrian, though, when all that's left is polished professionalism, they do.

Did I say the second set was to be treasured? I meant *most* of the second set. "New Minglewood Blues" is another over-amped waste of set-list space, "High Time" is movingly sung by Garcia but undercut by tacky keyboard textures, and the best thing that can be said about Weir's two-part "Lost Sailor">"Saint of Circumstance" is that at least they're playing something written somewhat recently. Then, just before launching into the next tune, Weir dedicates "He's Gone" to Irish Republican Army member Bobby Sands, who'd died the day before on hunger strike in a Northern Ireland prison. The Dead were still avowedly apolitical at this time and rarely dedicated songs from the stage (a recently deceased Neal Cassady in 1968 and a newly imprisoned Bear in 1971 are the only other dedicatees that come immediately to mind), but whichever side of the issue you're on, when someone starves themself to death for an idea, it can't help but make an impression. It's impossible to say if that's why much of the music that follows is so consistently inspired, but for whatever reason, it is.

"He's Gone" is creaky and a touch torpid, but that's okay, it rings true, and that's what matters most when it comes to elegies. The "Caution Jam">"Spanish Jam">"Drums" that materialize out of "He's Gone" is a jamming jamboree that lasts for a straight twenty-five minutes (okay, seven minutes are devoted to "Drums"). "Caution Jam" is more powerful for being a vocal-less jam and not the actual song, Pig's old showcase an unintended tribute to another fallen soldier. (Coincidentally or not, they'd never play it again.) By the time the group rolls into a tense and teasing "Spanish Jam," you'd almost think it was a different decade (except for the cheesy keyboards). After "Drums" and a short (3:56) but twisted "Space," "The Other One" into "Going Down the Road Feeling Bad" into "Wharf Rat" into "Good Lovin." All of them burn, even in pint-sized form ("The Other One" is less than six minutes long); what they lack in length they make up for in intensity and intention.

When it's all over, you wonder how they got there. It doesn't matter. They did.

12/15/86 – Oakland-Alameda County Coliseum, Oakland, CA

1: Touch of Grey; C. C. Rider; When Push Comes to Shove; Beat It On Down the Line; Greatest Story Ever Told; Loser; Cassidy; Althea; My Brother Esau; Candyman; Let It Grow

2: Iko Iko; Looks Like Rain; Black Muddy River; Playing in the Band>Terrapin Station>Drums>Truckin'>Wharf Rat>Playing in the Band>Good Lovin'

E: Johnny B. Goode

IN A 1981 television interview with Garcia and Weir, *Tomorrow* host Tom Snyder asked the pair how the Grateful Dead "managed to stay current." Weir pauses, looks at Garcia, then replies, "I don't think we've stayed current. I don't think we ever *were* current"; to which Garcia quickly adds, "Yeah, right. That's closer to the truth." The Dead outlived glam and disco and punk and New Wave and No Wave and every other kind of wave that was supposed to submerge them and render them musically obsolete, and that counts for something. Like the Ramones, another band that created an utterly singular style, the Grateful Dead existed in their own musical universe, regardless of the decade or the *Zeitgeist*, and countless Dead Heads attended their first shows during the 1980s and '90s and made lifelong friends and lasting memories and remain understandably attached to this era in the band's concert history. A friend of mine, the writer Jason Schneider, attended around twelve Grateful Dead shows in the 1990s, and what he remembers best isn't the music so much as the warmth, vibrancy, and inclusiveness ("C'mon in, we're all Heads here") of the other attendees. For him and his friends, Shakedown Street, the carnival-cum-vending scene that inevitably took place outside of wherever the Dead happened to be playing, was as much a revelation of good vibes and high spirits as the concert itself. Plus, people weren't afraid to look dumb and dance, something you weren't likely to find at a Neil Young show.

I get it. I know that the Violent Femmes' self-titled first album is better than its follow-up, *Hallowed Ground*, but I bought the latter first, so it's always maintained an extra-special place in my Femmes-loving heart. Besides, in his memoir, *Deal*, Kreutzmann recounts how, no matter how smacked-out Garcia was, or how much his declining physical condition compromised his playing and singing during this period, there were always at least a few minutes per show when it felt like it used to feel—like it was *supposed to* feel. But fond reminiscences and enduring friendships aside, three or four minutes out of a couple of hours isn't very satisfying musical math.

By the early 1980s, Garcia wasn't making much eye contact with his bandmates onstage anymore or listening to what the others were playing (to be fair, neither were they), and he often looked bored, in the one place he could usually count on being happy. Was it because of the progressively less-than-inspiring music or the heroin? What came first: the chicken or the skag? Regardless, at some point Garcia became a full-time, full-on heroin addict. In *Living with the Dead*, Rock Scully recalls how "by 1983 Jerry's life is reduced to chord books, junk, junk food, Häagen-Dazs, and cigarettes. Cocooning, he hides from the band. At gigs he locks himself in his dressing room. Afterward, we crawl back in our caves."

During this time Garcia successfully resisted several drug interventions by the band; suffered a diabetic coma and nearly died (his weight ballooning to nearly three hundred pounds); attempted and succeeded in getting clean a few times on his own, only to inevitably relapse; got married a couple more times; and basically followed the sad path of least day-to-day resistance. In the most chilling anecdote in roadie Steve Parish's memoir, *Home Before Daylight: My Life on the Road with the Grateful Dead*, Parish recounts how, when in 1984 his young daughter, his pregnant wife, and their unborn child were all killed in an automobile accident, Garcia offered his devastated friend some heroin, telling him it would help kill the pain. "In that instant," Parish wrote, "I felt more pity for Jerry than I did for myself, because he really was trying to help. He just didn't know any other way."

It took a diabetic coma to do what friends and family and common sense couldn't. Although getting busted, in January, 1985, for smoking heroin in his parked car, contributed to Garcia slowly weaning himself off the opiate addiction that had plagued him since the late '70s, it wasn't until he collapsed in his Marin County home in July of the next year, after returning from a long Grateful Dead tour through the better class of football stadiums, that the real transformation began. After the arrest, shows tended to be better because Garcia was better—more energetic, overall; more, if relatively restrained, jamming; more-committed singing and playing—but it was his collapse and hospitalization (including five days spent in a coma) that put him on the road to "real" recovery (Garcia would suffer drug relapses and endure a myriad of health crises for the remaining nine years of his life). After nearly dying, and having to virtually relearn how to play guitar, Garcia was committed to doing more with what time he had left than getting high and eating ice cream and watching TV and resenting the gargantuan scale of success that had become Grateful Dead Incorporated. The band stayed off the road for over five months while Garcia recovered and didn't play another gig until December 15, 1986. The opening song of the night was "Touch of Grey."

The Dead had been playing "Touch of Grey" since its concert debut over four years earlier, but never had this great little pop tune, a cranky mid-life-crisis song that somehow evolves into a catchy pledge of commitment and renewed purpose, seemed more appropriate. When Garcia sings "I will get by" in the chorus, you can feel the love and devotion that Dead Heads had for Garcia as they roar their rowdy approval. The same thing happens during "Candyman" when Garcia sings that the Candyman is back in town—a long, earnest bellow of adoration and support. Garcia claimed that the outpouring of concern he received from Dead Heads during his long convalescence, especially their letters, aided significantly in his recovery, and it's a couple of undeniably moving moments. Unfortunately, they're primarily non-musical moments. It was the group's first gig in nearly half a year, so the usual sort of rustiness could be expected—and they did get better as the night wore on, and even better yet over the course of the three Oakland shows, of which this was the first—but *better* doesn't necessarily mean *good*. 12/15/86 is wonderful drama. It's not wonderful music.

Remarkably, given the circumstances, there is some new music. Even more remarkable, it's courtesy of Garcia, who used the occasion of his celebratory return to the living Dead to unveil two recent Hunter co-writes. "When Push Comes to

Shove" is an agreeable rocker that sounds a little like "Tennes-see Jed," without the latter's distinctive rhythmic hiccup, and with words that recall "Run for the Roses," the excellent title track of Garcia's otherwise disappointing—and last—solo album from 1982. It's like a lot of latter-day Garcia tunes: sort of memorable, but mainly because it dimly reminds one of oth-er, superior songs. "Black Muddy River" manages to be moving, in spite of suffering from the same lack of melodic originality (it could be a thousand other midtempo pop-gospel tunes), a touching tale of someone on the other side of youth looking for—and finding—a reason to keep going, and is sung with great feeling by Garcia.

The raspy voice of conspicuously limited range that helps make the melancholic "Black Muddy River" as moving as it is can't be counted as a positive when it comes to every song, however, and although Garcia's voice would improve (margin-ally) with his health, it was never again the sweet instrument of subtlety and discovery it once was, the inevitable cost of smok-ing heroin and a couple of packs of cigarettes a day. Garcia's—and the entire band's—joy with making music again is obvious and enlivening to hear, but can't compensate for such a down-turn both vocally and instrumentally. (A one-armed Garcia is still a more tasteful and interesting guitarist than most fully functioning guitar players, but there's simply less going on when he solos now, as if the ceaseless musical curiosity and adventurousness of before has been partially chemically cas-trated.) When you're an ambitious young artist it's not only understandable, it's advisable to ignore your physical existence as much as possible, in order to fully devote yourself to what's most important: developing your craft. As one grows older, though, the every-year-more-crumbling corporeal needs to be more and more tended to. Without a relatively healthy body to accommodate it, the soul has no place to call home. Garcia wouldn't have treated his guitars as indifferently as he did his voice or his body.

The remainder of the show is pretty much archetypal '80s Dead: a few truncated old favourites, a mediocre newish song (Weir and Barlow's "My Brother Esau"), a couple of intermittently stirring Garcia ballads, a pointless cover tune or two, usually courtesy of Weir ("C. C. Rider"? Really?), and the inevitable upbeat encore. The show must go on.

3/29/90 – *Nassau Veterans Memorial Coliseum, Uniondale, NY*

1: Jack Straw>Bertha; We Can Run; Ramble On Rose; When I Paint My Masterpiece; Bird Song>Promised Land

2: Eyes of the World>Estimated Prophet>Dark Star>Drums>Dark Star>The Wheel>Throwing Stones>Turn On Your Lovelight

E: Knockin' on Heaven's Door

GRATEFUL DEAD APOLOGISTS will tell you that, while it's all good—*All eras are equal! Don't be a hater! Don't be an era-ist!*—some periods in the band's performing history are admittedly better than others. Like the spring of 1990. The Dead themselves must have thought so, too, compiling a double-CD set (*Without a Net*) from a number of shows played in late 1989 and early '90, and even consecrating the entirety of a single concert (3/29/90) to plastic several years after the fact (*Wake Up to Find Out*). It's a good choice. Not only does it contain all that's prototypical of the band in concert during the last epoch that even their most fanatical followers admit could be called exceptional, it also features a guest appearance by saxophonist Branford Marsalis, who inadvertently illustrated that it really wasn't so exceptional, after all.

By the spring of 1990, the Dead were, indeed, cookin' again, but more often than not on perpetual simmer. As the years rolled on and the venues got bigger and bigger (again), the shows became shorter and the performances safer, but with a commensurate increase in stolid professionalism. Which is precisely what is needed if your intention is to have a successful, lucrative career. Which the Dead obviously did. (All of the band's biographers acknowledge that Garcia was the most adamant about not playing mega-domes anymore and taking some much-needed time off to rest and work up new material, but the road to increasing artistic irrelevancy is paved with unacted-upon good intentions.) By the dawn of the twentieth century's final decade, the Grateful Dead were among the highest-grossing touring bands in the world, partially because of their outsider pedigree and nostalgic pull, and partially because they'd scored a top-ten single back in '87 with "Touch of Grey," their video of the same also having been a minor MTV hit. No one gets this big without doing their part.

How much had things changed since the first time the Dead played Nassau Veterans Memorial Coliseum, way back in 1973? At that point, it was seen as a necessary concession to the group's growing popularity and a cause for quality-control concern; seventeen years later, at least a hockey rink wasn't a football stadium. And the home of the Islanders was where the Dead were on March 29, 1990, in the midst of a long spring tour (to be followed a month later by a long summer tour, to be followed by...)

For most of the brief first set (seven songs!), the band's performance was about as inspiring as the concrete box where it was taking place. Granted, Garcia was relatively healthy, and friskier on stage than he had been for years, and yes, after a little more than a decade, Mydland's place in the band had become entrenched. Just as Keith had eventually affected the evolving sound of the band, so too did Mydland, his bright, busy keyboard work and workmanlike vocals keeping the band on an even keel and ensuring that, on any given night in any given city at any given multi-purpose arena or stadium, the group was, consistently, rarely less than competent. This is the age of the dependable Dead. Dependable is good when you're buying snow tires or listening to a weather forecast; it's not so good when your ostensible goal is to stir up awe and break open brainpans and pour iridescent illumination inside.

The only noteworthy numbers of the opening set, until the penultimate tune, are the year-old "We Can Run," a Mydland soft-rocker that wouldn't have sounded out of place on a latter-day Bonnie Raitt album, and "When I Paint My Masterpiece," another valiant, if futile, cover-tune attempt by Weir to spice up what had become a decidedly bland set list. Then they introduced a musical guest who was going to help them out on the next tune, Branford Marsalis.

The "Bird Song" that follows is everything that what had preceded it wasn't: multicoloured, many sided, and intent upon going where *it* wanted to go. When musicians speak of those rare occasions when "the music plays the band," this is what they're talking about. It probably helped that Marsalis and the Dead had never performed together before, let alone practiced; because the group members were forced to listen to each other (and their guest) for a change and not merely blast through rote versions of overdone songs there's an element of gamble and exhilaration, uncertainty and oomph. Here, as on the even-better "Eyes of the World" that opens up the second set, the tempo is more relaxed than usual, probably in the name of understandable performance anxiety, but resulting in more open space to play around in and explore. Marsalis is the undeniable focus for the remainder of the night (he hung around until the end, at the Dead's insistence), even adding his horn to a game version of "Dark Star," his smouldering sax taking Garcia's guitar's place as the musical hub.

But the MIDI mush the band occasionally employed these days to "expand" the sound of their instruments is, to me, dirty digital smog. And Garcia's voice is permanently shot. And too often it seems as if he's playing one note for every two he used to play. And...

But hey: how about that Branford Marsalis?

7/9/95 – *Soldier Field, Chicago,* IL

1: Touch of Grey; Little Red Rooster; Lazy River Road; When I Paint My Masterpiece; Childhood's End; Cumberland Blues; Promised Land

2: Shakedown Street; Samson and Delilah; So Many Roads; Samba in the Rain; Corrina; Drums>Space; Unbroken Chain; Sugar Magnolia

E: Black Muddy River; Box of Rain

AND TO THINK they'd played their first gig at a pizza parlour in front of a few supportive friends and a handful of pizza-pie-munching strangers. And that their friend Sue Swanson found it necessary to remind them to stand up when they performed, that this was rock and roll they were supposed to be playing, after all, not folk music. Just over thirty years later, if you were one of the 61,500 people packed into the Chicago Bears' home stadium to witness what would turn out to be the Grateful Dead's final concert, and if you had difficulty making out what was going on up on the postage stamp–sized stage, you could always watch the show on one of several gargantuan video screens. Then again, considering Garcia's alarmingly unkempt silver mane and pasty complexion and droopy posture, maybe not. Sometimes the past is best viewed through a glass darkly. Sometimes very, very darkly.

In the five years since the band's last musical peak (comparatively speaking), not much had gone right. Brent Mydland had died of a drug overdose, not long after returning home from the vaunted spring 1990 tour, and in their overeager attempt to keep the dream alive and the band on the road and the cash coming in, the Dead almost immediately hired Vince Welnick, the former keyboard player of shock-rock band the Tubes, to take his place. (Their first choice to replace Mydland had been Bruce Hornsby, who begged off becoming a full-time member because of a burgeoning solo career but nevertheless helped ease the transition by adding his acoustic piano and accordion to the mix, a refreshing breath of musical air amidst all of the technology the band had increasingly encumbered themselves with.) Everywhere they played, it seemed, fans without tickets were tearing down fences and facing off with cops and turning every show into a dance with destruction and a drug bust waiting to happen (a hit record, a popular music video, and a reputation for being the ultimate party band will have that effect). In the end, too many counterfeit Dead Heads (Dead Heads don't crash fences) fatally upset the fragile Grateful Dead ecosystem, crowding Dead shows with thousands of yahoos in backwards baseball hats who didn't know the difference between getting high and getting wasted. The glossy glare of the latter-day band's sound only encouraged less contemplative listening and more fist-pumping obliviousness.

Maybe that was for the best. Not even the biggest, most self-deluding Dead Head would make many musical claims for the band's final tour, a long trek through a hot, humid summer of endless anonymous stadiums crammed full of tens of thousands of rabble-rousing fans who were ready to slip on some tie-dye and hoist a few king cans and get down and par-*tay*. To be fair, although Garcia's physical deterioration and emotional absence were the principal reasons why there's very little salvageable music from this time, the other members of the band weren't doing a lot to compensate. Not that they didn't try.

Ever since the start of Garcia's slow eclipse in the early '80s, Weir had done his best to lighten the load and liven things up and keep the music moving, whether by goosing the set list with a variety of cover tunes or scampering around the stage or making up for Garcia's disappearing act by ensuring that his own voice was loud and clear. More importantly, he stayed fit and focused and provided a positive physical role model to his aging bandmates, most of whom were approaching the half-century mark (Weir, Kreutzmann, Hart) or had already passed it (Lesh and Garcia). Lesh, who admitted in his memoir, *Searching for the Sound*, to becoming an alcoholic around the time of the band's "retirement" in 1974, had quit drinking and dropped thirty pounds and was singing again, something he'd stopped doing after the "retirement" shows because of a throat problem. It's fitting that, although the highlight of the night is unquestionably Garcia and Hunter's moving "Black Muddy River," it's one of Lesh's rarely performed songs that wraps things up for good.

Until then, in addition to flubbed lyrics and off-key singing and tepid lead guitar, more of the same ("Cumberland Blues," "Promised Land," "Sugar Magnolia"); more new songs no one needed to hear (keyboardist Vince Welnick's abominable "Samba in the Rain," Lesh's only slightly less unnecessary "Childhood's End"); a couple of promising recent numbers (Weir's staccato-sassy "Corrina," Garcia's—no surprise here— melancholic "Lazy River Road" and "So Many Roads"); not much real jamming. Fittingly—again—the night's two big moments occur during the tour-ending double encore, concluding not only the concert but the Dead's entire career.

"Black Muddy River" isn't the most original-sounding song (although the chorus does, admittedly, stay with you), and maybe if it hadn't been Garcia himself singing it—and if one wasn't aware of the disquieting circumstances of his life and his death less than a month later (from a massive heart attack at yet another expensive rehab clinic, a week after his fifty-third birthday, his body battered by decades of bad diet, chronic smoking, and opiate-abetted general physical neglect), it's worth wondering how affecting it would actually be. Anyway, it is. It's very affecting. Painfully affecting.

And when the band kicks straight away into "Box of Rain," Hunter's timeless tale of death, acceptance, and love, Lesh's voice a croaky catastrophe but no less poignant for it, decades disappear and they're all clear-eyed kids again and Garcia asks Lesh if he wants to play bass guitar in this new group he's started. Just like Lesh sings, it's all just a dream they dreamed one afternoon long, long ago. A dream we're still dreaming.

BONUS TRACK

5/14/74 – Harry Adams Field House, University of Montana, Missoula, MT

1: Bertha; Me and My Uncle; Loser; Black-Throated Wind; Scarlet Begonias > It Must Have Been the Roses; Jack Straw; Tennessee Jed; Deal; Big River; Brown-Eyed Women; Playing in the Band

2: US Blues; Mexicali Blues; Row Jimmy; Weather Report Suite (i. Prelude; ii. Part One; iii. Let It Grow) > Dark Star > China Doll; Promised Land; Not Fade Away > Goin' Down the Road Feeling Bad > One More Saturday Night

AFTER A COUPLE of warm-up gigs, the squeaks and squalls have (mostly) been worked out and the Wall of Sound is finally ready to roll. The new album, which the band spent much of the spring recording, is done and dubbed *From the Mars Hotel*, their second LP for their very own fledgling record label, Grateful Dead Records. (The band's boutique label, Round Records, will release *its* first offering, Garcia's second solo album, *Compliments*, a week before *Mars Hotel's* appearance in a month and a half.) They were also back on the road, where the music always sounded best and the musicians felt most fulfilled, the second gig of a long spring tour that won't stop until it's a long summer tour that turns into a long fall tour. (Why not? They were all young and healthy and happy, and doing too much and moving too fast is what being young and healthy and happy is all about, isn't it?) It's a Tuesday night in Missoula, Montana, and it's good to be the Grateful Dead.

It's also 1974, which means that even the relatively straight-forward stuff in the first set has plenty of snap, crackle, and pop, including show starter "Bertha," which features an unusually assertive Keith on keys (he's delightfully ubiquitous all night) and everyone else leaning hard into a tough and fleet and fun (if vocally flimsy) opening number. "Loser" is eerie perfection; "Scarlet Begonias" (played a little fast, in only its second performance) has room for a short jam and a spirited Donna vocal workout before dissolving into a sweetly aching "It Must Have Been the Roses" (which gets its only fifth official airing); "Deal" burns, thanks to Keith and Garcia's tandem talents; "Big River" might be just another Weir cowboy-song cover, but Garcia shreds it with a fiery solo; and "Playing in the Band," to close out the first set, is sloppy in places, particularly during the reprise (it's the Dead, what do you expect?), but once it's airborne, it's twenty-one minutes of swirling, swaying, wah-wah-infused magic. "We're gonna take a short break and we'll be back in a few minutes, so everybody hang loose," Weir announces at song's end. Sounds like a plan.

Because the Dead are their own bosses now, and paying the bills, and it actually matters how many records they sell, they've slid toward the middle a little and done what pretty much every other rock-and-roll band in the land does when pushing new product: release a single, in the hope of getting it on the radio and encouraging album sales. Which could be construed as a trifle scary—What's next? A spot on the *The*

Midnight Special, right between Peter Frampton and Loggins and Messina?—but it's okay, after all, because the song is "US Blues," and if that's what constitutes selling out, then sign me up and slap a price tag on my ass, because who else but the Grateful Dead could make short and snappy and catchy sound so seditiously, sardonically leftfield?

With "Row Jimmy," things start to spread out a bit, to settle down and lengthen and linger, but as pretty and powerful as it is, it's "Weather Report Suite (i. Prelude; ii. Part One; iii. Let It Grow)">"Dark Star">"China Doll" that stops time and puts its interstellar stamp on the evening. The tender guitar chords that preface it, the pensive lyrics (supplied by songwriter and Weir associate Eric Andersen) of "Part One" that centre it, the textured tone and rumbling, racing rhythm that is "Let It Grow" itself: if this is the Dead's move to the mainstream, let's all jump in the water and paddle with the current together. Sixteen minutes later, when most bands would be towelling off and cooling down and inquiring of the assembled locals, "Hey, how's everybody doin' out there? Is everybody ready to rock?" the Dead ease into a titanic "Dark Star" that is '74 jazzy but still late-'60s skronky yet somehow moodily meditative as well. Garcia soars, Lesh does the same, Weir counterpoints and is ceaseless in coming up with intriguing chord combinations for Garcia to respond to (or not), Keith pops in and out and around and pulls it all together, and Kreutzmann keeps it going. At times, the music seems to melt, a Dalí painting created out of stopped watches and long-extinguished celestial bodies. And out of "Dark Star"'s concluding cacophony: the still fairly new "China Doll," the reassembling of order and the sweet worldly sorrow that accompanies all finite things lucky enough to live and die and wonder why they're not a deep breath of infinite deep space as well. *Phew*...

If, after fifty minutes of absolutely enthralling, otherworldly playing, you think it might be time to take it down a notch, or maybe even consider wrapping things up, you're not thinking like the Dead, who decide (after a pointless "Promised Land"— Chuck Berry wrote a lot of songs, folks—why not mix it up a bit?) that a scrumptious "Not Fade Away">"Goin' Down the Road Feeling Bad">"One More Saturday Night" medley might be a good idea. Their audience's heads out of the clouds now and everyone's feet back on the ground, it is. Dancing, after all, is what feet are for.

The only blemish on the entire night is the idiot who throws a plastic beer pitcher at the stage before the final number and hits Weir in the face. Sure, the crowd might be a tad bigger (eight thousand) than what's ideal, but who throws stuff at the stage during a Grateful Dead show? Must not have been a Dead Head.

HIDDEN TRACK

PICK A PRIZE – How I Became a Dead Head

FIRST SET

I COULDN'T RIDE the rides. Not unless I wanted to wear the corn dog, candy apple, and purple slushy I'd consumed almost immediately upon arrival at the annual Chatham Jaycee Fair. I was afraid of heights and suffered from motion sickness, so the Zipper and the Salt and Pepper Shaker and even the Ferris wheel were out of the question. And it wasn't as if I could pass the time strolling around the fairground holding hands with whomever I'd asked to go with me. Girls didn't go to the Chatham Jaycee Fair with boys who were afraid to take a trip on the Skydiver. I could have just not gone. I could have stayed home with my growing collection of *Hockey News* and my Elton John records, or I could have helped my dad cut and trim the lawn and bag the clippings and ... Of course I went. If I couldn't fly, I could at least overeat.

There were also games of chance and games of skill, but I didn't play games either. Not because they made me nauseous or dizzy, but because they didn't make good financial sense. Not only were games almost as expensive as rides—and the odds always stacked against you—but even if you did manage to get the ball in the hole or pop the balloon, I was thirteen years old, I didn't need a cute stuffed animal or a Kewpie Doll. But you can eat only so much cotton candy, and watch other people defy gravity for only so long, before the need to do something—anything—tops the desire to be fiscally responsible and carny-savvy. Besides, if you ran into someone from school, it was better to be seen shooting an air rifle or attempting to knock over a milk bottle than to be spotted wandering the fairgrounds, purposeless and Earthbound, girlfriend-less and gassy.

I won. I forget the game, I forget what I had to do to win, but I remember being surprised that I won. The guy with the handlebar moustache running the booth pointed at the wall of prizes, made it clear that I could pick any one item starting *here* and ending *there*, but nothing from *that* row or *that* row or *that* row. Thankfully, I wouldn't have to smuggle home an oversized stuffed bear or a pet rock; there were two entire rows of framed mini-mirrors, adorned with beer-company and rock-band logos. I didn't drink yet, so I didn't have a favourite brand, although the red-and-white Budweiser mirror was admittedly pretty nifty. BUDWEISER. THE KING OF BEERS. It was hard to beat being the king of anything.

"Let's go, pal, you're a winner, pick a prize."

There weren't any Elton John mirrors. There were Black Sabbath mirrors, Judas Priest mirrors, Van Halen mirrors, there were even Bachman–Turner Overdrive mirrors. Maybe the Budweiser mirror wouldn't be so bad. It was better at least than a Ted Nugent mirror. Who wanted to wake up to Ted Nugent every morning?

"Pick a prize, pal, I've got other people here who want to play, too."

"I guess I'll take the one with the skull."

"Good choice, here you go. Who's next? Who feels lucky?"

THE GRATEFUL DEAD. Another hammerhead heavy-metal band, no doubt. But a human skull with a lightning bolt in place of a brain *was* pretty cool. I'd hang it in my bedroom, on the wall above the Sears stereo I'd gotten for Christmas. I was a teenager now and heading to high school soon. It was about time I had my own stereo.

FRIDAY NIGHTS WERE for the grocery store, A&W, and the Woolco Mall, in that order. If my dad was in an especially good mood, we'd eat dinner at Ponderosa instead of A&W, where the price of your chopped steak and baked potato also included free Pepsi refills and the all-you-can-eat salad and sundae bars. When I was younger, my mum and I would take the bus downtown and deposit my dad's cheque from Ontario Steel in the bank and, as she liked to say, "have a look around." But once the Woolco Mall arrived—off Highway 40, where there used to be cornfields—no one went downtown anymore. That was okay. The Woolco Mall—no one called it by its actual name, the North Maple Mall, everyone called it the Woolco Mall—had everything.

Besides Woolco, the mall had the usual grown-up business-es—a shoe store, a pet store, a jeweller—but there were also places that were interesting even if you weren't looking for a new pair of sandals or goldfish food or cheap earrings. There was Leisure World, for instance, a little shop that sold models and board games, and a T-shirt kiosk, and a Coles books store. We'd always enter through the Woolco entrance and, before go-ing our separate ways, decide upon a time to meet back in front of the snack counter. My dad would usually head straight for Woolco's hardware section, my mother the women's clothing department, me, sporting goods. Recently, though, glistening new footballs and baseball gloves and rows of hickory-fresh hockey sticks had lost some of their consumptive lustre; now, I'd take only a quick tour of the sporting-goods section before heading out for the territories, the rest of the mall, where the really fun stuff was.

You weren't supposed to enjoy reading—reading was something you had to do for school—so I kept to myself my growing pleasure in lying in bed or sitting in a lawn chair and disappearing for hours inside a book. There were two book-stores in Chatham—the Coles downtown and the Coles at the mall—and they seemed to stock pretty much the same books, the same bestsellers and cookbooks and celebrity biog-raphies, but the Coles at the mall had something that the one downtown didn't: a discount bin full of remaindered books, each one bearing a telltale black-marker slash across its top or bottom edge, and usually costing about a third of the normal sticker price. This was where I'd discovered *About Three Bricks Shy of a Load*, Roy Blount Jr's behind-the-scenes account of life with the Pittsburgh Steelers, as well as *Rock 'n' Roll Babylon*, a nice and gory picture book chronicling some of popular mu-sic's most infamous flame-outs. You never knew what you'd find in the bin.

Grateful Dead: The Music Never Stopped. Well, well, what did we have here? Apparently, the Grateful Dead were more than just a framed carnival mirror; they were also a music biography. If they were anything like their name, I thought, this might be good, *Rock 'n' Roll Babylon* good. I paid for the book and start-ed back for Woolco. I was early. If my mum and dad weren't ready yet, that was okay, I had my book with me.

SAM THE RECORD Man was *it*, the only place in town to buy music. (Technically, there was Records on Wheels, another chain, in the Woolco Mall, but Sam's was bigger and had more records, and the people who worked there looked like they actually listened to music—and, c'mon, it was *Sam's*.) If a band or a musician mattered, they had their own little white plastic divider with their name written on it, if they didn't, they didn't. The Grateful Dead must not have mattered because they didn't have a little white plastic divider with their name written on it. Bobby Goldsboro and Grand Funk Railroad did, but not the Grateful Dead. (Which was likely why WRIF and WLLZ, Detroit's two de rigueur rock radio stations, didn't include the Grateful Dead in their playlists.) Which was no big deal, actually, since the band's music, as described by Blair Jackson in *Grateful Dead: The Music Never Stopped*, didn't sound like it was for me, wasn't of the catchy singer-songwriter variety I was used to. In recounting the band's history, Jackson wrote of half-hour-long jams and jazz-influenced guitar solos and unusual time signatures (whatever those were) and songs, when they *were* songs and not marathon improvisational vehicles, that weren't about being in love or falling out of love or looking for love, but about…well, it was hard to tell *what* they were about, at least by their titles alone. "Alligator." (Okay…) "That's It for the Other One." (The other *what*?) "New Potato Caboose." (Is this kids' music?) "The Eleven." (This *is* kids' music.) "China Cat Sunflower." (Huh?) "Weather Report Suite." (What the hell?) Whatever they were about, whatever they sounded like, they weren't "Crocodile Rock" or "Candle in the Wind," that was for sure. I knew what I liked because I liked what I knew, and the Grateful Dead weren't the sort of thing I liked.

I did like *Grateful Dead: The Music Never Stopped*, though. I liked it a lot. Which was odd, because although there were a few salacious rock-and-roll tidbits tossed into the author's tale (lots of drugs, especially L S D, and the death of one of the founding band members due to alcoholism), the book was mainly about music, about how five very different individuals with five very different musical skill sets somehow, through either luck or fate (take your pick), managed to find each other and collectively create a kind of music that wasn't like any other kind of music. Pour some bluegrass (courtesy of the lead-guitar player's banjo-picking past), folk (the rhythm-guitar player), blues and R & B (the keyboardist), rock and roll (the drummer), jazz, and even weirdo avant-garde stuff (by way of the bass player, who'd never played the instrument before being asked to join up because, unlike the group's previous bassist, he "understood music")—pour it all into a great big bowl, toss in plenty of psychedelics, and let simmer during the Summer of Love until it tastes not quite like anything you've ever tasted before.

But where were the groupies? Where were the stories about driving motorcycles down hotel corridors and sinking Cadillacs to the bottoms of swimming pools? In their place was something called "A Critical Discography," an album-by-album analysis of the band's entire recording history. I didn't know you were allowed to treat unserious stuff like rock music seriously; I thought being serious was only for boring things like school or politics or religion. There was also a short section entitled "The Best of the Grateful Dead Taper's Choice," a breakdown of the most important Grateful Dead concert recordings, which wouldn't have been available at places like Sam the Record Man even if the band *had* had their own little white plastic divider with their name on it. How did people get them, then? *Why* did people get them, if, as described in the book, the shows were recorded by audience members on portable tape recorders, and the sound quality was often subpar? I liked that I didn't know the answers. I also didn't know why I liked it, and I liked that, too.

I also liked a good bargain, and Sam the Record Man had their own discount bin full of records with punch holes in their corners and $1.99 stickers slapped on their cellophane covers. *Barry Manilow Live. Firefall. The Beach Boys Love You. Shaun Cassidy. Blues for Allah. Liona Boyd: The First Lady of the Guitar.* Hold on—*Blues for Allah*? Why did I recognize that title? I picked up the album. Oh, right: *Blues for Allah*, by the Grateful Dead. The cover portrait, a red-robed skeleton sporting bug-eyed red sunglasses and playing a violin, was, I thought, a pretty good indication of what the music inside sounded like (I'd graduated from being an Elton John fan to a Neil Young fanatic by this point, so bug-eyed skeletons weren't an encouraging musical sign), but I was in grade eleven now and had a part-time job as a busboy at the Wheels Inn, so what the heck, it was only two bucks. It seemed kind of lame to have a mirror with a band's name on it hanging on your bedroom wall and not own at least one of their albums. Besides, it would be fun to listen to the record after reading again what the review in my Grateful Dead book said. Among other things, it referred to the title track as "obtuse." The next time I was at Coles, it looked like I'd need to buy a dictionary as well.

IT MUST NOT be easy for people who weren't alive during the 1970s and '80s, before the World Wide Web, to understand how difficult it was to find what you were looking for, particularly if you grew up stranded in suburbia and didn't know what you were looking for. You knew you wanted more music in your life—better music, or at least *different* music—but unless you were lucky enough to have an older, wiser sibling or an equally hip friend, you usually had to rely on the radio, which in Chatham meant Detroit stations, which meant a steady diet of what is now called "classic rock" but back then was just the same old bands and the same old songs played over and over again, the same Zeppelin, Stones, Sabbath, latter-day Floyd, et cetera, with a few local favourites—Mitch Ryder, J. Geils, the ubiquitous Bob Seger—thrown in to give the station's corporate shell game a veneer of disc-jockey authenticity. There was the CBC as well, the country's national broadcaster, but I felt even less affinity for it; the shows that did feature contemporary music sounded less like rock-and-roll programs than like adult-education classes in good taste. I may not have known much about music or art, but I had a pretty solid hunch that good taste had very little to do with either. In fact, I was pretty sure that, if anything, it was the opposite of the real thing. I'd pillaged my parents' battered record collection before I was old enough to have a single album of my own, and Little Richard and Jerry Lee Lewis, among others, were a lot of things—loud, horny, vivacious, sometimes scary—but tasteful wasn't one of them. Art without *A-Wop-Bop-A-Lu-Bop-A-Wop-Bam-Boom* wasn't art.

Before the internet, you needed people. A high-school friend's older, slightly taciturn brother was my source for a slew of fresh musical discoveries—Lou Reed, the Stooges, Bob Dylan—and only because, being hearing impaired, he played his stereo so incredibly loud that when I walked past his bedroom, on the way to my friend's room, I could hear Iggy's motor-city roar underneath his headphones. As expected, *Blues for*

Allah hadn't been quite my cup of musical tea (some of it was almost melodic enough to remember the next day, but the beat never stayed in one place for long, the words didn't make much sense—when the songs *had* words and weren't winding instrumentals—the lead guitar player played solo after solo, and the title track wasn't, after all, *obtuse* but, I thought—with a little help from the *Concise Oxford Dictionary—opaque*). Even so, I couldn't help bragging (and lying) to another high-school friend that, among a bunch of other bands he'd probably never heard of, I was also kind of sort of into the Grateful Dead. So was his mother, he said, and offered to lend me one of their albums from her collection. Once I got over my disappointment that I wasn't cooler than Brad Langford's mum, I was thankful. Even if, like the Grateful Dead LP I'd bought at Sam's, her album turned out not to be nearly as good as any one of my increasing number of Neil Young records, it was something else I'd never heard before, somewhere else I'd never been. All you had to do was turn on the radio to know how rare that was.

WHAT WAS IT with this band and album titles? First, *Blues for Allah*, now *History of the Grateful Dead, Vol. 1 (Bear's Choice)*. Who was *Bear*? The album didn't say. Musically, at least, this was more like it. Gone were the twisting song structures and long instrumental passages of finger-blistering complexity, and in their place were one side of acoustic songs and another of loud, rude blues. But (there were a lot of *but*s with this band) the acoustic side was pop-music peculiar, wasn't full of crisp guitars and pretty harmonies and instantly hummable tunes about romantic relationships but, instead, weird old folk songs, sloppy, out-of-tune vocals, and bashed-out, barely together accompaniment (at one point, one band member can be heard asking another if he wants to play "Dark Hollow," to which his bandmate replies, "Do you know the words?" You wouldn't hear *that* on a Crosby, Stills & Nash album). On side two the electric instruments were broken out and things got a little livelier but no less slapdash, the two very long blues workouts (both in excess of ten minutes) sounding like the entire band was stuck in quicksand and trying to jam its way out of the sonic sludge. I didn't ask my friend if his mother had any more Grateful Dead albums I could borrow.

SECOND SET

AFTER NEIL YOUNG, to greater or lesser degrees of fervent devotion: early Bruce Cockburn, the Doors, the Velvet Underground, Gram Parsons, the Byrds, Willie P. Bennett, Gene Clark, the Beach Boys, John Hartford, John Stewart, Little Feat, Karen Dalton, John Prine, Ronnie Lane, Muddy Waters, Richard Thompson, Townes Van Zandt, plus assorted other minor musical deities (Paul Siebel, Willis Alan Ramsey, Son House, Gillian Welch and David Rawlings, Michael Nesmith, Sister Rosetta Tharpe, Gary Stewart, Alex Chilton, Lucinda Williams, James Booker, the Deadly Snakes, Duster Bennett, Nick Drake, Hound Dog Taylor, the Staple Singers, Kevin Ayers, John Martyn, Syd Barrett, Bert Jansch)—and plenty of others for whom I'd need to go to the CD shelves or the record racks to remind myself of the sundry joys delivered and the aural epiphanies provided. I studied philosophy as an undergraduate, did a graduate degree in creative writing, and ended up being a fiction writer who composes books of non-fiction between novels, but music has always been at the foundation of everything I've written. "All art constantly aspires to the condition of music," Walter Pater wrote. All of *my* art, anyway, whether it succeeds every time or not (or, for that matter, at all).

Music has not only underpinned how I write (for the ear, then the toes, then the brain), it's also frequently been my ostensible subject, whether in novel form (*Moody Food*, among others) or non-fictionally, as in *Lives of the Poets (with Guitars)*. In both cases, the kind of music I've written about has typically been in the country-rock, or at least Americana, camp, steel guitars and big sideburns and high-lonesome harmonies dominating. It was inevitable, then, that I'd eventually get around to the Grateful Dead's two 1970 albums, *Workingman's Dead* and *American Beauty*, the group's own characteristically skewed take on rock-and-roots-and-roll. The carnival mirror that I had hanging on my bedroom wall as a teenager was long gone by then (it disappeared when I had for university a couple of decades before), as were my Grateful Dead book and vinyl copy of *Blues for Allah*, but once more I found myself in the company of the Dead.

Anyone who's heard either one of these records—and who, if they're interested in country-rock at all, hasn't?—knows what an absolute delight they are. Talk about catchy—just *try* and stop singing along to the chorus of "Uncle John's Band" or "Casey Jones" or "Sugar Magnolia." Struggle in vain to resist the cracked cosmic charm of "Ripple," the propulsive pluck of "Truckin'," the charming backwoods yarn that is "Friend of the Devil." These are simply great songs, each one assiduously stuffed with compelling lyrics, memorable melodies, and plenty of dexterous picking. I was in the habit back then of burning mix

CDs for myself and my friends (Twang #1, Twang #2, et cetera, eventually making it all the way up to Twang #30-something), composed of my favourite country, rock, blues-rock, and country-rock tunes of the moment, and it was no stretch to slide the Dead's "Dire Wolf," say, right between the Flying Burrito Brothers' "Sin City" and Wanda Jackson's "Let's Have a Party." Maybe it was time I checked out the Grateful Dead one more time, beyond its twin, turn-of-the-decade masterpieces. Maybe there were more twangy treasures waiting to be discovered.

Nope. Well, yes, there undoubtedly were a few more excellent songs, but for every "Bertha," the surprisingly sprightly lead-off track to the live *Grateful Dead* (a.k.a. *Skull and Roses*) album I picked up, there were epic noodle-fests like "The Other One" and even, God forbid, drum solos. *Drum solos.* Jesus H. Christ. Almost equally off-putting were songs like "Wharf Rat," which, frustratingly, I couldn't penetrate, I couldn't figure out. Ballad? Gospel? Spooky soundtrack to an Alcoholics Anonymous confessional? What the fuck? It was undeniably moving, in a minor-key, nebulous sort of way, but it didn't make sense. Whatever it was, I knew it wouldn't work sandwiched between the Byrds' "Mr Spaceman" and Gary Stewart's "I See the Want To in Your Eyes." Oh, well. It looked like I was done with the Dead. Again.

IT'S RARE TO fall in love after the age of forty. Which makes sense. Habits harden, curiosity cools, enthusiasm atrophies. I fell in love with the sound of Jerry Garcia's guitar when I was forty-seven years old. I'd always adored the Hammond B-3 organ—Jimmy Smith's sturdy soul-jazz albums were about as close to jazz as I got, because if I couldn't hum it, I couldn't hear it—and by chance I came across a used album credited to

Garcia and organist Merl Saunders, *Live at Keystone*, featuring just them with a drummer and a bassist. It was used, it was only fifteen bucks, it was an original pressing, why not? It was the same reason I'd selected the mirror at the fair. The same reason I'd bought *Blues for Allah* at Sam the Record Man. The same reason I'd told my high-school friend, whose mother lent me her Grateful Dead record, that I was a fan of the band when I wasn't. *Chance* and *luck* and *why not?* are good enough reasons to fall in love as any.

I can remember where I was (in the green Naugahyde reading chair in our library-cum-listening room). I can remember what I was drinking (cheap Portuguese wine). I can remember listening to the long, utterly mesmerizing guitar solo Garcia performs on the album's final cut, "Like a Road," and thinking, *I need to hear every note of music that this man ever played.* Maybe it was because in his solo band the emphasis was necessarily on Garcia's guitar and vocals, and there was none of the near-symphonic contributions of the other members of the Grateful Dead to occlude his gift. Maybe it was because it simply took me that long to grow the ears to hear it. Regardless, I was hooked. Hooked on the sound of Jerry Garcia's guitar.

Garcia's guitar tone, his instrumental DNA, was delicately, powerfully, swoop-and-soar sinewy and inimitably his, his ceaseless musical curiosity compelling him to eschew guitar-solo clichés and squeeze out the full emotional range of almost every note he played. I'd listened to rock and blues and hard country most of my life, and I could appreciate a tasteful, economical guitar or keyboard solo as much as the next person, but the prolonged exhibition of instrumental virtuosity had always been something you waited to be over with until you got back to the song and the words. But Garcia's guitar had a personality; Garcia's guitar *talked*—was alternately thoughtful, playful, melancholy, ethereal, anguished, obstinate, joyful, bewildered, blissful, and oftentimes all of these things over the duration of a single ten- or fifteen-minute song. They couldn't be any shorter. It would be like asking Monet to paint a pond full of water lilies on the inside cover of a matchbook.

I POSSESS LITTLE to no willpower. This was why I couldn't memorize the periodic table in high school and failed chemistry class and why the to-do lists my wife helpfully leaves around the house for me rarely get done. If I want something, however—if I *need* it—I will get it, or at least work hard and long enough to get close enough to get a good look at what I think I'm missing. To experience the depth and breadth of Jerry Garcia's genius, you have to listen to him live (like John Coltrane or Miles Davis or Duane Allman or any other genuine musical auteur dedicated to improvisation), and at twenty minutes, tops, to an LP side, that's simply not a big enough canvas for Garcia to compose his aural pictures. The Grateful Dead is most Dead when it's live. To properly appreciate the band, then, you have to either go the bootleg route or stock up on Dick's Picks or Dave's Picks or Road Trips or any of the other posthumously released, officially sanctioned concert recordings. Which I did. And continue to do.

In the house of the Dead there are many mansions, and I don't like crowds or the smell of patchouli and I don't wear tie-dye, so that isn't the kind of fan I am. For me, it isn't about anything but the music, particularly the sound of Garcia's guitar (and, to a lesser degree, his much-underrated vocals). Whenever the world, in all of its deflating, awful ordinariness, is too, too much with me and I need a transcendental transfusion, all I usually have to do is play some Garcia, I know his guitar will hook me up to the infinite, will take me for an extraterrestrial joyride I frequently don't want to return from. I need to hear it fairly regularly or I risk endangering my fragile sense of otherworldly wonder.

My name is Ray, and I'm a Dead Head.

ENCORE

FIVE YEARS AGO, a few years after I became a Jerry Head, I was going through an old dresser in my parents' basement when I found the Grateful Dead mirror I won at the fair forty-something years before. I don't think anyone had even looked at it in three decades. It was like it had been waiting there for me.

I also found my Indian Creek Road Public School 400-metre first-place badge and a pair of brown leather pants, waist size twenty-eight and Jim Morrison low in the hips, that I wore just once, to the second of only two times that my high-school band performed in front of actual people other than ourselves.

It would take more than a badge to get me to run four hundred metres now. On the other hand, if I ever managed to shed those pesky seven or eight inches around the waist, maybe I could get the band back together. I put the badge and the pants back where I found them. The mirror I took home with me.

It's hanging on the wall behind me as I type this.

It all rolls into one...

RAY ROBERTSON is the author of nine novels, five collections of nonfiction, and a book of poetry. His work has been translated into several languages. He contributed the liner notes to two Grateful Dead archival releases: *Dave's Picks, Vol. 45* and the *Here Comes Sunshine 1973* box set. Born and raised in Chatham, Ontario, he lives in Toronto.